'I DON'T MIND THE SEX, IT'S THE VIOLENCE'

Film Censorship Explored

'I don't mind the sex, it's the violence'

FILM CENSORSHIP EXPLORED

Enid Wistrich

MARION BOYARS · LONDON

A MARION BOYARS BOOK
distributed by Calder & Boyars Ltd
18 Brewer Street, London W1R 4AS

First published in Great Britain in 1978 by
Marion Boyars Publishers Ltd
18 Brewer Street, London W1R 4AS

ISBN 0 7145 2534 0 Cased edition
ISBN 0 7145 2535 9 Paper edition

Printed in England by
Hillman Printers (Frome) Limited, Somerset

CONTENTS

INTRODUCTION
WHY FILM CENSORSHIP MATTERS

Film is the last of the media in our country still subject to
the ancient repressive control of prior censorship and given
the force of law by government regulation. That control is
the most expressive tribute which can be paid to the power
and impact of the moving, talking picture. The realism,
immediacy and topical relevance of social drama films, the
violent fantasy and potent imagery of crime, western, and
horror films, the eroticism of the romantic and more
explicit sex films all arouse strong emotions touching on
painful half-forgotten and repressed memories and dreams,
disturbing the papered over facade of everyday workaday
lives. They are a reminder of the world that was perhaps
once, that might have been, that could be. They threaten
our personal stability and our carefully constructed
defences. They substitute the possibility of chaos, disturbance and revolution for stability and order; of joy, beauty
and fulfilment for an ugly and drab existence; of tran-
quillity and hope for a racked and meaningless life; of
violence and death for life itself. The language and impact of film is immediate. Literacy is not required for
comprehension. Films are easily accessible, either on television or at local cinemas. Film-going is not socially
exclusive and indeed many middle class people place
it low in their list of arts patronage. Film is often still
regarded solely as cheap, mass entertainment, inferior to
the theatre as an artistic medium. Yet the recent
attempts of playwrights and producers to present old
classics in modern settings and to confront and involve
their audiences by various techniques suggest that the
theatre is conscious of its many limitations as a medium

and is striving to achieve some of the impact and effect which comes more readily to film.

In 1968, Parliament was persuaded to enact the Theatres Act which put the theatre into the most most favourable position in relation to censorship of any medium. Not only was the ancient office of the Lord Chamberlain which had been responsible for the prior censorship of plays since Elizabethan days abolished, but the Act prevents private legal prosecutions and allows proceedings to be taken against stage plays and shows only by the Attorney-General. In such cases a jury has to decide whether the play has a tendency to 'deprave and corrupt'. The Theatres Act came about because the theatre had become accepted in establishment circles as a respected artistic medium. Actors had risen from the status of strolling players to potential knights and dames, producers and directors from commercially minded impresarios to recipients of Arts Council grants. The Joint Parliamentary Committee which examined theatre censorship found that both the Arts Council and the Archbishop of Canterbury, twin pillars of respectability, favoured an end to prior censorship of the theatre (although eminent Catholics and the Free Church Federal Council did not).[1] The expense of theatre going, the location of theatres in city centres and the need to reserve seats meant that the audiences were overwhelmingly middle class. It had become safe to emancipate the theatre because its patrons were 'well educated' and largely adult.

The cinema has never achieved the respectable status of the theatre. Cinema going is still a far more casual habit and a cheaper one. The local cinema is liable to be filled with pensioners and truanting school-children in the afternoon, young men and women in the evening and families at weekends. It is a natural centre for troublesome adolescents, lonely bedsitter livers, and courting couples.

[1] *Report of the Joint Committee on Censorship of the Theatre*, H.M.S.O., 1967, Appendices.

8

The cinema auditorium is a dark, anonymous environment where there is little feeling of social occasion. The audience covers all social classes, but the group least represented are the middle aged and middle income; thus, precisely those who are in positions of authority and influence are least likely to patronize the cinema. Cinemas frequently remain in the respectable consciousness as doubtful social venues and by implication films are a doubtful form of entertainment. One of the commonest criticisms against cinemas (and one which is largely unjust) is that they never show wholesome family films.

The case against prior censorship of films has therefore never seriously been considered. The desire to control the entertainment of the young, the poor, and those thought to be socially inferior (including women) has been persistently strong over the centuries. In Regency England, for example, the Society for the Suppression of Vice, organised by William Wilberforce, initiated 623 successful prosecutions for breaking the Sabbath laws in the years 1801-2 alone, and these included dancing, fair entertainers, naked sea bathing and obscene pictures.[1] Even in the mid-twentieth century, the prosecuting counsel in the *Lady Chatterley* Trial was capable of asking whether jurymen would like their wives or their servants to read the famous book.[2] The cinema is identified as the entertainment of the masses, without superior characteristics or patrons, and therefore, the proper subject of control.

The other side of the coin is the dark one. Precisely because films are so powerful, so capable of evoking disturbing images and fantasies and repressed emotions,

[1] E.P. Thompson, *The Making of the English Working Classes*, Penguin Books, 1968, p. 442.
[2] C.H. Rolph (ed.), *The Trial of Lady Chatterley*, Penguin Books, 1961, p. 17. 'You may think that one of the best ways you can test this book ... is to ask yourself the question ... would you approve of your young sons, young daughters – because girls can read as well as boys – reading this book. Is it a book that you would wish your wife or your servants to read?'

the need to impose restrictions is seen as both urgent and desirable. A vital medium, popular classless patronage, an anonymous local social venue – all add up in the establishment mind to a suspicious and potentially dangerous environment. Hence the present situation. Controls which would be seen as intolerable for any other medium of communication or entertainment are accepted and the pressure for even stricter controls is pervasive.

Such an anomalous situation frequently has comic results. *O Calcutta*, the first of the successful stage shows to feature a frank and irreverent attitude to sex was running in the west end of London at the same time that the British Board of Film Censors decided to ban a film of the show from cinema screens. While coachloads of citizens from all points of the country came to see it on stage, it was forbidden on their local screens. The film still remains uncertificated by the BBFC although it received a local licence to play in the London area in 1974. *Emmanuelle* and *The Story of O* are highly erotic books published and available in Britain. Yet the two screen versions both met with censorship. The film *Emmanuelle* was only certificated after extensive cuts had been made to the original. *The Story of O* was banned completely in 1975 in spite of its admittedly discreet visual presentation. The attempt to prosecute the book *Inside Linda Lovelace* failed in the courts when a jury decided that it would not 'deprave and corrupt'. But *Deep Throat*, the film in which Linda Lovelace appeared, the making of which is amply described in the book, never even got as far as the censors; the customs officers banned its entry into the country under the powers which they have to prevent the importation of 'indecent' articles.

Since the advent of television cinema attendances have fallen steadily. If the middle aged who were accustomed in their youth to romantic, musical and western films now visit the cinema they are surprised to find that the crime is more violent, the love scenes more explicit, and the division between cops and robbers a good deal shadier than the films they remember. But the films which show 'bent' policemen and vicious cowboys reflect the loss of confidence and certainty in our present society and respect for its leadership figures. Scepticism about 'our' side in war since Vietnam, about 'our' political leaders since Watergate, and about the greatness of 'our' country since the decline of the pound do not provide a climate in which the confident assertion of traditional authority figures can be made. If the film's uncertainty is part of our own, the strident cries for the old films stands for our wish to return to the naivety and innocence of the past.

The explosion of sexual frankness is equally hard for people to absorb. As the modesties of the past are swept aside, many feel an outrage to their concept of privacy and decency. Others may envy the young their freedom and less inhibited behaviour. Again these concerns are projected onto the films which reflect the greater sexual freedom of our time. Men who previously condemned their own strong impulses feel guilty when they are openly aroused by erotic screen material. Women fear the more open expression of men's sexual fantasies and implications for their own sex since so many films scenes are designed to appeal to male sexuality and a part of the male fantasy appears to be the treatment of women as trivial sex objects and their subjection in the sexual exchange. The ambivalent or hostile attitude of women may indeed remain as long as sex scenes in films are designed, however inadvertently, for the arousal of men. The confusion of both sexes at a time of uncertainty about sexual roles goes a great deal towards explaining the success of Mary Whitehouse as an older 'nanny' figure re-asserting the values of reticence and inhibition. Her castigation of the new sexuality and its manifestations serves both to reinforce and to assuage the guilty feelings which accompany the pleasure gained from the films. The eagerness with which her prohibitions are welcomed represent a longing for reassurance, authority and certainty, however ill-informed, in an area where there is much embarrassment, fear and worried concern. In the same way, the evangelists of the Festival of Light provide an affirmation of faith and purity in an impure world.

Films both reflect and build on contemporary reality. Their excesses are our own and their evolution of ideas stimulate us to acceptance or rejection. The medium does not often lend itself to thoughtful or balanced presentation of conflicts. The typical radio or television use of documentary film and 'balanced' discussion is inappropriate. Film relies on a dramatic form highlighted by the technical possibilities of camera and cutting room skills. It is rarely the straight-forward documentary or the conventional crime film which offends. The greatest outcry invariably accompanies the most brilliant films which make the maximum impact. The cries of outrage following Kubrick's *A Clockwork Orange* were a tribute to its power and provocation. Calls to ban it may be read as a need to stifle and suppress its disturbing message. The seriousness and artistic quality of this film have never been in question and the British Board of Film Censors allowed it a certificate, but that did not stop police, judges, and newspapers up and down the country from attributing every local crime to its influence, and some local councils from banning it from their local screens.

The struggle over film censorship is thus a reflection of the most agonising conflicts concerning both the individual and our society. In deciding whether to censor, how to censor, and above all *what* to censor, we are saying more about the mores and the workings of our society than we may care to admit. That is why the subject, so frequently trivialised and sensationalized in the press, is worthy of close and serious examination.

THE RELUCTANT CENSOR

In April 1973 I was elected to the Greater London Council. That year the Labour Party recaptured control of County Hall after six years of Conservative majority. The Labour victory marked the end of an era of planning dominated by property speculation, office building and a powerful urban road building lobby and opened up the discussion of urban policy to very different perspectives, where the priorities of community and environment, traffic restraint and public transport came to the fore.

The new focus of concern accorded well with my own interests. Planning and transportation had always been prominent in my earlier Borough Council career and was certainly equal to my other strong interest in the field of arts and leisure services. It was my modest ambition to contribute to the GLC's key role in planning and transport questions in London. Accordingly, when I was asked to indicate my preferences for Council Committees after the election, I put Planning and Transport first and Arts and Recreation second.

Perusing the list of Committees and Boards and their functions, I was surprised to find one entitled *Film Viewing Board* whose functions were stated to be 'The viewing of films, the grant or refusal of consent for their exhibition, decisions as to category of films, control of publicity for films, and matters related to the exhibition of films.' In so far as I had ever given the matter consideration at all, I had always thought that film censorship was carried out by the British Board of Film Censors whose brief imprimatur on the screen preceded the roaring of MGM lions, the swinging of 20th Century Fox searchlights and other stirring introductory images. I had no idea that local authorities were in any way involved. Brief enquiry among more knowledgeable colleagues indicated that membership of the Board entailed attendance at the exhibition of 'dirty' films and was regarded as a bore, a giggle or a dubious 'perk'. I quickly decided that the viewing of 'blue' films did not fall within my range of local government interests and when I came to the column on the form I filled out for Council committee preferences headed 'Committees you do *not* wish to be considered for', I had no hesitation in putting a firm cross against 'Film Viewing Board'.

After the election, I faced a great volume of background, introductory and information papers from County Hall. As I worked my way through the envelopes, one small one of a thicker and more expensive paper caught my eye. I opened it and read an invitation from the Leader of the Council to become Chairman of the Film Viewing Board. I was stunned. In the handout of jobs, I knew my chances as a 'new girl' were slim. My hope was that someone might remember the posts I had held with Camden Council as Chairman of the Libraries, Arts and Recreation Committee or as Vice-Chairman of Planning, and would feel that I had some merit as a person to whom an appropriate office might be entrusted. To be offered 'dirty' films seemed to me to be a bad joke. And besides, as I thought about it, film censorship seemed an archaic exercise with which I did not wish to be associated. So I went around to several Councillors that I did know on the selecting committee asking them why on earth they had picked on me. Well, came back the reply, we decided that we ought to have a woman because the anti-pornography crusaders are always asking 'Would you take your wife to see this film?', and someone suggested you. They might have added what I soon came to realise, that the job is about the lowest on the list to be filled and, having made nominations to all the important, responsible and interesting posts, they were hard put to find anyone for this one. It was not exactly flattering and I decided to write a polite note of refusal.

But as I did so, several thoughts came into my mind. The first was a feeling that there was something illogical about the situation in our society that allowed books to be printed and plays to be performed freely but which required local Councillors to sit in judgement over film shows. I remembered the controversy in the 1960s before the passage of the Theatres Act when every playwright and producer was locked in argument with the Lord Chamberlain's Office about how many swear words he could include in his text. That fuss had all quietly disappeared after the Theatres Act came into force and the theatre had not been flooded by sex acts and bad language. I asked myself why films should be differently treated and could get no convincing answer. I began to feel that the matter should be explored more deeply and that the position of Film Viewing Board Chairman might give me the opportunity to do so. The second thought was a good deal more prosaic. I was in no position to play hard to get for any other job. At that stage it was film censorship or nothing. The combination of intellectual curiosity and political realism won and I wrote a letter of acceptance instead.

May 4 saw the first meeting of the newly elected Council. We all felt the meeting to be an important occasion when the new Leader of the Council would tell the people of London on our behalf what the policy of our administration was to be. I did not know that news of appointments to Committee Chairmanships were made known to the public that day. The phone rang as I was about to leave home and I was asked by a newspaperman what I thought of my new job. I was surprised at his interest but replied that I thought film censorship was not really a job for local authorities and that the whole system was anyway archaic. He seemed very interested in my reply. When I reached County Hall and approached the Council Chamber I was rather worried that I would not find my seat there in time as a bell had started to ring to give notice of the start of the meeting. A group of newsmen and photographers was waiting with an official who

15

stopped me and asked if I would mind saying a few words to them on my new job. I replied that I really could not as I had to enter the Council to hear the Leader's statement, but they were so insistent that I felt obliged to repeat to them what I had already said to someone else on the phone. As I left the Chamber a few hours later, I was told of more requests for newspaper and radio interviews and started to get worried. Then I saw an evening paper whose front page had a banner headline 'Enid – London's Film Censor' and a photograph with a full report on what I had said, plus details of my age, my family and the significance of my remarks to the London film scene. The Leader's statement of policy for London was well down the page. When I reached home that evening, I found my children wide-eyed with excitement. They flourished more copies of the evening papers. The phone, they said, had been ringing non-stop with enquiries from the newspapers. A lady reporter from the *Sun* had arrived begging for an interview and was waiting in the front room, and a photographer was to follow. I was appalled, my husband amused. We decided to send the lady reporter away for an hour, took the phone off the hook and sat down to family supper. Then I repeated my piece for all and sundry callers. By the next day, I was still in a state of shock but beginning to understand. Serious proposals for London's future were, it seemed, of less interest to the media than the censorship of 'blue' films. As news, a woman film censor was streets ahead of a reasoned statement by the Leader of Britain's largest and newly elected Council on planning and housing. And my tentative opinion, which seemed plain common sense to me, was highly controversial. What had I let myself in for?

In the weeks that followed, I began to make enquiries about the role which local authorities played and found it a great deal more complicated than I had supposed. Accident, coincidence, and evolution had contrived to produce what Herbert Morrison had described as 'a curious arrangement', adding with characteristic national smugness, 'The British have a very great habit of making curious arrangements work very well, and this works.' However, although bans on particular films receive a lot of press coverage, few people know exactly how the 'curious' system of censorship does work. When movies first began there was no censorship, but public concern was centred on the fire risks inherent in the showing of highly inflammable nitrate film in premises not built for the purpose. Several disastrous fires led to the enactment of the Cinematograph Act of 1909 which gave local authorities the power to license premises used for film shows, with a view to enforcing adequate fire regulations. It was not long however before the licensing powers were used for other purposes. In 1910 the London County Council made a condition of its licence the restriction of Sunday film shows. Challenged in the Courts, the judgement was made that the Act allowed local councils 'a discretion as to the conditions which they will impose, as long as those conditions are not unreasonable'. Censorship was considered a 'reasonable' condition, and thus was local authority censorship born.

The cinema trade for its part was anxious for its reputation and for protection from arbitrary censorship actions by local authorities. It set up its own censorship body, the British Board of Film Censors, in 1912 with a former reader of plays for the Lord Chamberlain as its President. The hope was that the Board's decisions would win local authority confidence and be adopted by them, but when local authorities continued characteristically to retain their independence of action, the industry began to press for a government appointed Board of Censors with legal powers of its own. In 1916 the Home Office actually announced its intention to establish such a body but later that year a change of Home Secretary led to a reversal of the policy and the retention by local authorities of their powers. In 1920 and '21 two leading local authorities, Middlesex and London County Councils, were the first to make it a condition of their licences that the British Board

17

of Film Censors' certificates should be adopted. The pattern now established was that the BBFC, a body responsible only to the industry, carried out the actual censorship, but its certificates were given legal validation and impressed on the public by local authority licensing powers.

Although local authorities may impose censorship, they are not obliged to except in relation to children. Indeed it was only in 1952 that the duty to censor films for children was laid on local authorities, and the Cinematograph Act of that year laid no such obligation on Councils to censor films for adults. Nor can local authorities delegate their function of censorship entirely to the British Board of Film Censors. It is always open to them to override the BBFC's decisions by censoring films with a BBFC certificate or by licensing a film without one.

In practice, the local authority role is therefore a vestigial one. Since local councillors have neither time nor inclination to see all films, they adopt the BBFC certificate for the great majority without question. But many do take sufficient interest in films which have aroused controversy to review them and to ban them, often on the flimsy evidence of press reports. Some others will review and license films without a certificate. The BBFC therefore watches the actions of local authorities closely and trims its decisions accordingly. If it is to retain the industry's confidence, it must keep the number of independent local authority actions down to a minimum. But, although the actual role played by local authorities is marginal, the existence of local authority licensing powers is crucial to the operation of the system. Without them the BBFC's certificates would be purely voluntary and no cinema need observe them.

A further curiosity of the system until very recently was the immunity which films had from legal action. Holding that films were subject to a separate system of control, Parliament omitted films from the Obscene Publications Act of 1959 and the Theatres Act of 1968, with the exception of film shows held in private houses. Attempts made to prosecute *Blow Out* and *Last Tango* under the Vagrancy Act and the Obscene Publications Act in 1973 and 1974 respectively failed, and only in 1975 was a private action under the common law offence of 'outraging public decency' allowed. The removal of their immunity stung the film industry into action and, as a result of their pressure, films have been brought under the Obscene Publications Act, but the consent of the Director of Public Prosecutions is required before actions can be taken.[1]

Another anomaly is the position of cinema clubs which are exempt from local authority licensing powers although they may still be subject to prosecutions at law. The clubs by-pass prior censorship and were therefore the target of the Cinematograph and Indecent Display Bill of 1973 which sought to bring them within local authority jurisdiction, but that Bill fell with the Conservative government. The commercially run cinema clubs are, however, widely tolerated as purveyors of 'pornography' to the 'dirty raincoat' brigade. The tolerance appears to be similar to the acceptance of call girls as a part of human 'vice' and weakness. Just as brothels and prostitution arouse relatively little hostility compared to permissiveness and promiscuity, so the commercial sex film clubs are accepted while sexually frank films on general exhibition are not.

The Greater London Council is the most significant local licensing authority in relation to film censorship. There were 234 licensed cinemas in the GLC area in 1975, approximately one seventh of the total in the country, and these included all the West End cinemas, many 'art' cinemas and the Soho cinemas which show a milder version of the kind of film seen in the cinema clubs. The GLC is considered to be the custodian of 'liberal' censorship, licensing films which the BBFC feels to be too extreme for national certification but which might be tried

[1] See Criminal Law Act 1977.

first under a London licence. *The Language of Love*, a Swedish sex education film, was first licensed by the GLC in 1970, and the GLC's action was followed by a number of other local authorities until, eventually, the BBFC itself felt it safe to give it a certificate.

In 1965 the GLC agreed to an amendment in its rules of management which moved away both from the Home Office model rules and from its own previous rules. The earlier rules of the former London County Council, like the Home Office rules, prohibited the exhibition of films 'offensive ... to public feeling'. The LCC rules also banned films which were held to be 'injurious to morality' as well as those which would 'encourage or incite to crime', 'lead to disorder' or contain 'any offensive representation of a living person'. Alec Grant, a barrister who became Chairman of the new GLC's Film Viewing Committee in 1965, succeeded in putting through an amendment to the rules which changed the basis on which the censorship of films was to be considered. Arguing that since the enactment of the Obscene Publications Act of 1959 the censors of film should use the same criteria as those now applied to the printed word, he proposed that the test now to be applied was whether the film shown had an effect 'which is, if taken as a whole, such as to tend to deprave and corrupt the persons who are likely to see it'. The tests of morality and offensiveness were both struck out. A second new test was added to bring the rules into line with the legislation on race relations, namely, that films should not 'stir up hatred against any section of the public in Great Britain, on grounds of colour, race, or ethnic or national origins'. The change in the rules was significant because it acknowledged that the same tests should be applied to films as to other forms of expression, rejected the view that the ability to offend was a basis for censorship, and that a public body should attempt by censorship to control the morality of its citizens. The new rules were adopted by the Council without a division and were retained when the Conservatives won a majority at the GLC elections of 1967.

20

The early 1970s saw the 'backlash' against the liberalising trend of the 1960s. The Festival of Light formed in 1971 called for a nationwide campaign for purity and decency. The National Viewers' and Listeners' Association set up in 1966 at first concentrated its efforts on television and radio. Lord Longford set up his own Commission of enquiry which published a 'report' on pornography in 1972 advocating a legal standard which would prohibit material which would 'outrage contemporary standards of decency or humanity accepted by the public at large'.

The reaction was also felt at the GLC. In 1972, the Council was pressed to ban both Ken Russell's *The Devils* and Stanley Kubrick's *A Clockwork Orange*. Although it was not the usual practice to view films which had been granted a BBFC Certificate, the then chairman of the Film Viewing Committee, Dr Mark Patterson, agreed that the Committee should see *Clockwork Orange* and said that 'We are going to have to consider the social and political implications of certain films'. Of *Clockwork Orange* he said, 'Personally speaking, I thought it a superb piece of cinema which had an important message; but in the context of the violent times we live in it was unsettling.' His interviewer, Alexander Walker, commented that 'Dr Patterson was at pains to stress that political censorship was not sought by his sub-committee but I formed the impression that its members disturbed by chaos in Ulster, the Aldershot outrages and violence in the picket lines during the miners' strike are tending to sharpen and harden their attitude to films that reflect anarchy without providing answers – or like *The Battle of Algiers*, advocate violent revolution.'[1] The GLC took no decision to ban either film after viewing them. In the same year the film of *O Calcutta* was banned by the BBFC and presented by the distributors for a licence to the GLC. The Film Viewing Committee accepted a cut version of the film, but the decision was requisitioned to a full meeting of the Council where,

[1] *Evening Standard*, 29/1/72.

following a vigorous campaign by the Festival of Light and their allies, the Committee's decision was revoked by a handsome majority of 62-30. The leading campaigner, the Conservative Councillor Frank Smith, pushed further in March 1973 when he attempted to get Bertolucci's film *Last Tango* reviewed with a view to banning it. The decision was again referred to the full Council but this time the decision was in favour of the status quo and the Film Viewing Committee's decision was upheld.

The GLC was not, however, at all happy about the law and practice of film censorship and particularly its own role in the system. In May 1972 the Council formally requested the Government to set up an enquiry into the law and practice relating to film censorship. In March 1973, it repeated the request and asked that, if the enquiry warranted the continuation of censorship, 'a more appropriate executive body than local authorities' should be used to carry it out. Both requests were rejected by the Conservative Home Secretary Robert Carr who was reported by the Home Office to hold the view that '... the Home Secretary is by no means persuaded that the present system, which has served the public well in the past has developed by experience, is incapable of adjusting itself to the strains now being put upon it, or that anything else more acceptable could be substituted for it. In particular, he is not convinced of the desirability of relieving local authorities of their ultimate responsibility in a matter in which circumstances and attitudes are likely to vary considerably in different parts of the country and wider considerations may need to be tempered by a certain responsiveness to local feeling.'

When the new Greater London Council assembled in May 1973, the film censorship position was thus in deadlock. Pursued by the Festival of Light and the controversy surrounding recent films, the Council had turned to the Government for help and been turned down. They were instructed to soldier on in the front line of a task which many felt to be onerous, distasteful and full of contradictions. Such was the position when I was appointed Chairman of the Film Viewing Board.

Once I had accepted the job, I began to enquire about the way in which the system worked and soon became aware of its many complexities. It was also clear that few people at the GLC liked the Council's involvement in an area which aroused much controversy and embarrassment and was felt to be far removed from the other legitimate spheres of local government work. It was accepted wearily as a distasteful chore, a kind of white man's burden which had to be carried out. There were the inevitable anti-vice 'crusaders', balanced by a small group of determined liberationists ready to pass (almost) anything and another one of conscientious 'liberal' censors anxious to be broad-minded about sex, but not to excess, but professing concern about the content of violence in films.

My enquiries had not gone far before I discovered that the duty of censoring films for adults was not obligatory. The solution to the burden which no one wanted was therefore clearly to stop censoring for adult audiences. Although the Obscene Publications Act unfortunately did not apply to films, I was assured that there were several laws which could be brought into use should some really unspeakable outrage appear on London's screens. Our withdrawal from censorship seemed to me to be a straightforward and justifiable way of bringing the Council's involvement to an end which would allow freedom from prior censorship while still providing a final safeguard for the nervous, in the form of proceedings in an open court of law. Every way I looked at it, it seemed right. The Council could continue to validate film certificates which restricted the access of children to 'X' films, and it could use its powers to control front of house publicity in order to prevent garish photographs and posters unwelcome to the public. There was, it appeared, a simple and elegant way of solving a problem which everyone had been fussing over for so long. Moreover, I discovered that the Greater London Regional Council of the Labour Party, the regional party which backed the new majority group on the GLC, had that very year passed a resolution opposing all forms of censorship and recommending that 'the Greater London Council should under no circumstances impose censorship'. Armed with this knowledge, I therefore wrote a short paper urging my party colleagues to consider seriously a policy of waiving its permissive powers to censor films for adults. Realising that there would inevitably be doubts and worries about the effects of a basic change of practice, I suggested that we should first carry out consultations with a number of official and interested bodies to see if there were cogent objections to such a proposal, examine the research evidence on the 'harm' caused by films, and commission a survey of public attitudes to film censorship in London to find out if our proposed action would broadly meet with public support. Since the Government had twice refused the Council's request to carry out an enquiry into film censorship, we could carry out our own enquiry to see what justification remained for the system and for our own role in it.

The Council's officers were startled by the radical approach shown and a few found it difficult to disguise their own feelings of antagonism to the ideas propounded, but, under the leadership of the senior officer, they accepted the obligation to assist members in forming and carrying out policy and recognised that there was a vacuum of professional 'advice' in this particular area. Moreover, the notion of the Council ceasing to implore the Government to act but carrying out its own investigations no doubt appealed to local government officials and indeed provided that element of continuity with past policy and experience on which they so much rely. The Council had also been much plagued in the past by claims from the Festival of Light that it spoke for the 'silent majority', and a survey of public attitudes would at the very least establish the truth of that proposition.

Meanwhile, it was suggested to me that we should take advantage of the Home Office's offer to the Council of

24

consultations and that I should also meet and discuss censorship with the Secretary of the British Board of Film Censors. These two meetings which it was probably thought would soften my attitudes were more influential than any other factors in confirming my opposition to the system. Had the people I met impressed me with their wisdom and superior judgement, I might have accepted that they had a platonic role to play as the guardians of the values of a good life. Instead I found in the Home Office only a stuffy and complacent orthodoxy of view, while the BBFC Secretary, perhaps seen on an off day, seemed to offer only a weary defensiveness in relation to his role. Most infuriating of all was the patronising attitude which was adopted. The senior Home Office official advised me to see a few of the unpleasant films which he was sure I would not like before forming any conclusions. Stephen Murphy of the BBFC was equally convinced that I should be sickened by what I saw and offered to show me some violent horrors from his special collection. The inference was that once the little lady had seen the naughty films, she would be so shocked that she would fall back on the big strong men for protection. That approach did not go down well. I have never appreciated condescension from men.

The proposals suggested were duly presented to the Film Viewing Board in June 1973. It was clear that those members who had only recently been pressing for a stronger degree of censorship than practised at present were appalled at the sudden change of atmosphere. The Film Viewing Board's defensive stance of the previous year had switched dramatically and they showed their alarm. However, the decision was taken to carry out discussions with relevant organisations on film censorship and to commission a survey of public attitudes before considering again the Council's future role in censoring films for adults.

2

VIEWING FILMS AT THE GLC

The GLC had always been considered in the film scene as the 'liberal' appeal board for the British Board of Film Censors. If the Board turned down a film or proposed too many cuts in it, the distributor knew he could appeal to the GLC for a viewing. If he was given a London certificate and the film did not cause a public outcry, he would then go back to the BBFC and argue for a nationwide BBFC certificate.

Moreover, it was understood that low cost explicit sex films found a ready market in the Soho area for visitors to London, and that the GLC might be prepared to certificate them on that basis. The system was cosy and well understood, with many a nod and a wink between the BBFC, the distributors, and the GLC. The justification given was that films which might cause offence in the puritan outback of the English and Celtic regions would be more easily accepted in the swinging, permissive metropolis. The football supporters 'up for the Cup', the business men in London to visit head office, the tourist in search of a little sinful amusement, might all have their dose of naughty entertainment and then return to their wives and homesteads of irreproachable respectability.

The great majority of the films which the GLC Film Viewing Board was called upon to view fell within this category. They were obviously cheaply made films with a very limited story line, characterisation, series of sets and locations. Most were made in Germany or France and the German ones often had the additional embellishments of heavy 'humour' with a distinct scatological preference. The general standard was so low that the Viewing Board's sessions became a struggle for its members between impatient disbelief and amusement at the feebleness of the material. *The Sex Life of the Three Musketeers*, for example, interspersed its amorous episodes with shots of the musketeers supposedly riding on their horses to another venue, but so bad was the filming that the actors were clearly jogging uncomfortably on wooden horses and the directors omitted even to make the background move. In another saga, *The White Slavers*, which attempted to invoke the atmosphere of the Middle East to which a girl was meant to have been abducted, the scene switched from a small room which was supposed to be in a brothel to shots of several surprised looking camels in the desert, clearly culled from a travel film. *Toilet Talks* concentrated its attention as the title suggests on the lavatory and included many shots of ladies and gentlemen in squatting positions thereon. The peak of its story line was an episode of sexual intercourse taking place in a lavatory.

While the background of these films was poor and scanty, the sexual content was invariably contained within very strict and accepted conventions. Someone, somewhere had a set of guidelines which were scrupulously followed. As far as I could judge, they appeared to be the following:

1. Full female nudity was acceptable, and indeed normal.
2. Male nudity was rare and in particular male genitals would only be shown at a distance and never in erection.
3. Kissing was confined to certain zones of the body. The kissing of women's breasts by men was, for example, allowed. The kissing of genitals, either between heterosexuals or homosexuals, was not shown but might be implied by vague and long distance shots. Naked women were shown kissing and fondling each other, but not men.
4. The position adopted in heterosexual intercourse was the orthodox 'missionary' one.

27

5. Sado-masochism in the sex act was not shown but might be implied by the presence of whips and other accoutrements of punishment.

The prototype formula sex film typically showed as its 'hot' sequences episodes where women were naked and fondled by men still wearing clothes, culminating in simulated intercourse which showed the man's now naked backside going up and down on top of the woman. Clearly the films were intended primarily for male stimulation but were confined within certain limits felt to be acceptable to the British market. From the obvious and frequently clumsy cuts that had been made, it was apparent that other sequences had been cut out by the distributors before submitting their films for a licence. The films were thus no more than a series of untidy chopped up episodes strung together in a loose story which could be viewed without alarm or outrage and with a pleasing sense of naughtiness by any self respecting adult male leading a respectable family life.

The titles of the films provided the biggest stimulation of all. *Techniques of Love*, *Teenage Love*, and *How to Seduce a Virgin*, for example, all promised more than they could be said to deliver. In their plastic world, the title was the come-on never fulfilled. Teenagers and virgins were all too clearly experienced ladies in their thirties and the 'techniques' shown invariably adhered to the usual formula. In short, these films were a consumer article tailored to the market. They gave the maximum of promise and titillation and the minimum of delivered goods, and they never departed from the implied view that sexual activity was something wicked but exciting outside the conjugal link and had nothing to do with warm or lasting personal relationships.

Such films, then, formed the staple diet of films which appeared before the Viewing Board. It used to interest me that they were often accepted by some of the members who were otherwise censorious of explicit sexual show. Very often it appeared that the triviality of the material and the underlying concept that the activities therein were 'naughty' made these films more acceptable than other quality films with a more serious treatment. To accept these cheap little articles could show that you were a 'good sport' without prejudicing a conventional moral stand. It was rarely the 'sexploitation' films that provoked real controversy on the GLC Film Viewing Board.

Another type of film which came before the GLC Film Viewing Board was the violent action film. Some were Kung Fu films which were more violent than usual, others were a string of violent episodes loosely hitched together, and a few were overtly sado-masochistic. The tendency of the Board was more strongly against such films than the sex films and it was an accepted convention among members that violent films were to be more readily refused because if sex was a 'Good Thing', violence certainly was not. Consequently, most were turned down for London certificates. I always used to anticipate such films fearfully, having a notoriously squeamish stomach, but I found the Kung Fu films too outlandish and fantastic to be really frightening. One Italian film, *Bay of Blood*, which the Board turned down, contained 13 murders one after the next, with dollops of tomato ketchup blood, but none of the episodes, or the sum of them, seemed to me to reach the suspense and horror of quite conventional murder and mystery films, and it kept within rigidly defined conventions. *Mark of the Devil*, again turned down by the Board, had a fair amount of unpleasant sadism with sexual overtones. Also rejected was *Love me Deadly* which included necrophilia, murder, and torture enough to turn a number of my colleagues green, and which I was fortunate enough to miss.

It was, therefore, a relief when the Board was occasionally asked to view a film of quality and serious intent. Such an event was unusual because the big distributors by and large accepted the role of the British Board of Film Censors and worked within its rules. Arguments would go on between the Censor and the film makers about the cuts the Censor wished to make. Part of the bargaining process was a threat by the film maker to take his film to the GLC. The Board used to receive a number of applications for viewing which were later withdrawn as the film makers and the Censor reached accommodation. But occasionally the film maker would revolt and carry out his threat, to the upset of Stephen Murphy who was reported as saying in 1971 when it was proposed to submit Makavejev's *W.R. – Mysteries of the Organism* to the GLC for a licence, 'I don't mind the GLC certificating dirty little films we turn down, but I *do* mind the GLC certificating an important, interesting and, as we are all agreed, not salacious film which has attracted a good deal of attention.'[1]

Such an upset between censor and distributor gave us the opportunity to view Ferreri's *Blow Out (La Grande Bouffe)*. We also saw an uncut version of the Andy Warhol *Heat* and the Henry Miller story *Quiet Days in Clichy*. Two smaller quality films made abroad but turned down by the censor which came to us were *Manson* and *More about the Language of Love*. We passed them all with 'X' certificates.

Blow Out was a clever French film which set out to shock and outrage not so much with its sexual episodes but by an emphasis on eating and over-eating which was intended to illustrate the decadence of food-conscious French society. The sexual scenes, which included some variations from the orthodox, were implied rather than explicit. The censor's chief objection to the film was the scene where one of the characters loses control of his bowels and releases noisily both wind and faeces and the lavatory also overflows. He wanted to cut these scenes to make it as he thought more acceptable to British audiences. It was evident that he had no intention of turning the film down altogether. This film was the first to which we applied a

[1]G. Phelps, *Film Censorship*, Gollancz, 1975, p. 87.

new policy of requiring the exhibitor to provide a story outline and a warning notice in the foyer. In spite of this, it became a special target of the anti-pornography 'crusaders'. Mary Whitehouse and Frank Smith visited the film and staged a walk out for the press with cries of 'It is totally disgusting ... the most revolting film I have ever seen.'[1] Mrs Whitehouse later tried to sue the film exhibitors under the provisions of the Vagrancy Act relating to indecency in a public place, but lost her action in the magistrates' court because that Act was held not to apply to film exhibitions.

Heat was a Warhol film to which the BBFC had earlier given a certificate after 4 minutes had been cut. The cuts annoyed the distributor, Jimmy Vaughan, who decided to resubmit the film uncut to the GLC. The censor's objection concerned two episodes of masturbation by a mentally retarded young man which were thought to be exploitative of the youth's condition. Vaughan on the other hand challenged his viewpoint, and wondered whether the scene would have been passed had the actor been playing the part of a genius such as Bertrand Russell. This particular argument seemed to me to show quite clearly how censorship imposes certain social values. The censor's no doubt well meaning attitude was that a mentally retarded young man should not be shown as having active sexual desires which were met by masturbation. Watching the film, I found it difficult to understand the objection. The young man was treated naturally and pleasantly by all the people around him who were well aware of his limitations. He was accepted fully by them along with his occasionally bizarre behaviour and his masturbation. Such an attitude seemed to me to be infinitely preferable to that overprotection and sentimentality towards the handicapped which can mask both fear and hostility and which denies them full acceptance as individual human beings. I felt that the censors were imposing their own erroneous social judgements on the public by cutting those scenes out.

[1] *Daily Mirror*, 28/12/73.

Quiet Days at Clichy was a Danish film based on the novel by Henry Miller which was turned down by the BBFC in 1970. It concerned the sexual exploits of two young men in Paris, one of them based on Miller himself. The film's characters were amoral in a most literal sense. Any opportunity for sex which presented itself was pursued without regard for relationships but with considerable wit and humour, and the treatment was strictly from a male viewpoint. In the version we saw a good many cuts had clearly been made, but there was still enough explicit sex to upset the censor and indeed to lead one member of the Board to say that the film was 'hard pornography'. I thought at the time that it could well cause trouble from enraged 'crusaders' but to my surprise it was shown without any scene or demonstration against it.

Of all the films that we saw, the refusal of the BBFC to pass *Manson* caused me the most surprise and concern. The film was a serious attempt to explain the life style of the Manson 'family'. It contained filmed interviews with several members of the 'family', including Lynette 'Squeaky' Fromme, later would-be assassin of President Ford, who discussed their feelings for Manson and their lifestyle. Interspersed were scenes showing the old farm where the family lived and something of their way of life there. Other scenes showed Manson at the time of his trial, some of his own statements and those of his followers. Several brief and unsensational references were made to the Tate-La Bianca murders, but there was no attempt to invoke the murders in an atmosphere of horror or to re-enact them. Apart from a few swear words used by the participants, we could see no reason for objection to the film. It was the prototype serious documentary which would have been well received on television. Several of our members felt it would make excellent material for discussion by teenage groups. The censor's rejection of the film was on the grounds that it made the hedonistic life of the commune attractive and rejected normal social values, and that the horror of the murders became unreal. Such a judgement could only be the product of fear that the lifestyle of the communes was so attractive that it would undermine 'normal' values, if not lead directly to further bizarre murders. Yet any sober reflection would show that the Manson family was an extraordinary pathological phenomenon, with Manson himself in an almost unique role of the mad leader who inspired total loyalty and sexual submission from his many women followers. The evil fascination exercised by Manson over women was powerful indeed, perhaps comparable only in modern times to the hold that Hitler exercised over his followers. A comparison with the earnest endeavours of commune livers was about as valid as comparing the normal political party with the Nazis. Oddly enough, at the time we saw the film, television was showing a series on the life of Hitler and the Third Reich which was presumably thought safe because Hitler was dead.

Our decision to pass this film brought out *The Times* at its best level of pompous pontificity. Although no one on the staff had seen the film, it did not inhibit the leader writers from saying under the headline 'A film to be reconsidered', 'It is legitimate in principle to argue that a film may be a very valuable document for study, yet too disturbing for general exhibition even to adults. It need not be overtly violent to be potentially dangerous in its effects ... The Manson affair is a particularly sensitive one, for in the publicity given to the original trials it was already possible to see how it evoked a reaction of appalled fascination that might well lead in some to imitation.'[1]

Although the film received a certificate in 1974, it did not receive a London showing until 1977when it was seen briefly and uncontentiously at the Essential Cinema. Meanwhile the BBFC had certificated *Helter Skelter*, a film which re-enacts both the trial and the murders with actors and which has been said by the Deputy Secretary of the BBFC to have 'very unpleasant scenes' in it. In spite of the

[1] *The Times*, 27/10/73.

contrast in treatment, the BBFC still prefers the fictional and violent treatment to the sober documentary one which it alleges 'glamourises the Manson family to a degree that could make their way of life seem very attractive to certain young people.'[1] The Manson family itself do not appear to share this view; the murder of Lawrence Merrick, the director of *Manson*, following threats by the family and their sympathisers, is thought to be their work.

More About the Language of Love was an unusual film for the Board to see because it was clearly intended as sex education. The Swedish participants included a lady who was supervisor of the Swedish Government Sex Education programme, a member of the Royal State Commission for Sexual Education, and two psychologists who were authors of a discreet and well read manual on sexual practices. Its 97 minutes consisted largely of filmed discussions between the psychologists and various people with problems of a sexual nature. Frigidity and impotence, subjects rarely mentioned openly, were discussed together with suggestions for overcoming them. Venereal disease also received calm consideration. The sexual needs of the handicapped, another normally taboo subject, were also brought into the film. The culminating sequence of the film was a depiction of actual sexual intercourse in a totally straightforward and graphic fashion. With cameras mounted from all angles, it left absolutely nothing to the imagination and no one seeing it could be in any doubt thereafter as to how the sex act was carried out. The choice of two beautiful young people and the addition of stirring symphonic music might be said to add an air of glamour to the proceedings, but the dedication to straight heterosexual sex could not have been more marked.

The censor's objection to the film was not to the explicit nature of the final sequence but ranged vaguely around a feeling he evidently had that some sequences were exploitative rather than educational in intent, meaning that he

[1] *The Guardian*, 1/10/77.

felt that they were included for sexual stimulation rather than instruction. The distinction is a difficult one to make in a film as explicit as this one. If intercourse is fully and graphically shown, can it fail to be stimulating in its effect? A discussion of the practices which might help in overcoming impotence is bound to lead to a desire on the part of the impotent to carry them out. The 'pure' sex education film in the censor's terms would appear to be a depiction of the sex act which made it appear neutral or even unattractive. The censor also objected to the sequences relating to the handicapped, feeling them to be inappropriate to the public cinema. To my mind, he was again reflecting the difficulty that many people have in accepting that the handicapped have sexual desires and needs.

The reception of *More About the Language of Love* by the Board showed how deeply divided opinion could be. To the majority, the film was straight sex education, a film which could only be helpful in leading couples to a happy and fulfilled sex life. Yet several of our members felt disgust and horror at the explicitness of the final sequence. Although discussion on these occasions was reticent, it later became apparent that a brief depiction of the couple kissing each other's genitals prior to the act of intercourse was felt to be perverse and highly objectionable. This particular incident was one reason why Raymond Blackburn and Lord Longford complained about the film and possibly also why the decision was taken by the Director of Public Prosecutions to prosecute it. It was a straight question of sexual mores with one group seeking to prevent the showing of what they felt was a disgusting sexual practice. A clear majority of the Board disagreed with this view. The Board's discussion did not however end at this stage. A group of the members argued strongly that the film should be given an 'AA' certificate so that it could be seen by teenagers. When the matter went to a vote, I found myself in the position of having to decide the issue from the chair as there was an equal division of opinion between members. I was in agreement with the view that the film

35

could indeed be helpful to teenagers, but it was also clear that a film thought by some to be outrageous even for adults would be doubly suspect for young people. Choosing prudence rather than conviction, I therefore opted for an 'X' certificate.

More About the Language of Love was put on at one of the cinemas dealing in the normal run of 'sexploitation' movies. It received no complaint whatsoever until Raymond Blackburn chose to visit it, returning for a second viewing with Lord Longford. The two lodged a complaint with the police and doubtless after many pairs of policemen's boots had trooped through the auditorium, the decision to prosecute the film as an 'indecent exhibition' was taken by the Director of Public Prosecutions. It greatly saddened me that the action was taken and that the jury found the charge proved. The heterosexual sex act, carefully and accurately depicted, could evidently be considered indecent, where allusion, insinuation and innuendo which carried the message that sex was an ugly business went unscathed and accepted in certificated films.

Two other films which should be mentioned are *O Calcutta* and *Snow White and the Seven Perverts. O Calcutta* was a film version of the American stage show which had been successfully transferred to London. The film had been the subject of earnest debate in the Greater London Council just before I became a member. It had been seen by the Film Viewing Board and accepted by the majority after cuts had been made in 1973. The minority then asked that the full Council take a decision on the subject and the decision was reversed.

When it became known that the new Film Viewing Board was taking a more permissive line than its predecessor on films with sexual content, the distributors wrote to us asking for a review. I was not enthusiastic about a restaging of the former battle but agreed to put the matter before the Board. Since several other distributors whose films had been turned down previously by the BBFC and the GLC had also written to us, we had to consider at what intervals we were prepared to view them again. We decided to put a two year embargo on reviews, with one year for exceptional circumstances. As *O Calcutta* was in the curious position of having been passed by the Board but rejected by the full Council, we felt it qualified for exceptional treatment. We duly saw the film in the cut version which the Board had earlier agreed and passed it, and it was again requisitioned to the Council and this time passed by thirty-seven votes to thirty-two. *O Calcutta*'s distinctive feature was its humourous treatment of sex. There were a series of skits which made fun of the trendier preoccupations with research into sexual behaviour, male phantasies and fetishes, and husband and wife swopping. It included several attractive dance scenes where the young men and women were shown nude but was otherwise discreet in its exhibition of nudity and the sex act. The acknowledgement of women's active participation and enjoyment of the sexual role was a refreshing change. It was one of the few films we saw which put men and women on an equal footing in the sex relationship.

Snow White and the Seven Perverts was an animated cartoon film which parodied Snow White's adventures with a version of sexual escapades. The interest of the film was the full rein the makers were able to give to sexual phantasy. Giant penises sprouted and stretched for miles until they found their quarry, breasts burgeoned and blossomed, and intercourse was energetic beyond all conceivable powers. The film was funny enough to cause great gusts of laughter among Viewing Board members. Not long afterwards, I was interviewed by a journalist and remarked that 'We all fell apart laughing' when the film was seen. When it was exhibited, I was amused but horrified to hear that my remarks were quoted in the publicity hand-out for the film as a kind of testimonial. After that experience, I was very cautious to keep clear of comments of this nature to the press.

Although we were frequently told that if we passed films which had been refused a BBFC certificate we would be opening the floodgates to great tides of filth and porn, the films we passed did not prove to have the irresistible appeal that might have been supposed. In the period May 1973 to the end of October 1974, the Board passed 20 films with an 'X' London certificate, but only 12 had been publicly exhibited at a London cinema by the end of 1975. Cinema exhibitors make their choice of films on the basis of what will best draw audiences, and their lack of interest in nearly half the films which we passed shows that the patrons are not so enthusiastic about poorly made sexploitation films and Kung Fu sagas as the moralists fear. Who has ever seen a queue outside a Soho sex film cinema? Big commercial successes can of course come from films with a high content of sex and violence, but they are likely to be well made films whose appeal rests on the credibility of the story and the quality of the acting. The longest queues of all are formed when a film is labelled as scandalous or controversial by the press. It is doubtful whether *Last Tango*, in spite of Marlon Brando, would have achieved more than the customary success of an 'art' film without the long campaign of the Festival of Light against it.

3

INVESTIGATIONS INTO THE SYSTEM

Once the decision had been taken at the GLC to carry out our own investigations into the Council's role in film censorship, we were able to research the background of film censorship and to begin a series of interviews with the people and organisations involved. Our role was a pioneering one, as we rapidly discovered. Few books had been written on the subject[1] although it was included cursorily in several studies of censorship and the obscenity laws. No government committee had ever sought to review the organisation, law, and practice of film censorship, let alone its effects or the justification for it. Lord Longford's privately constituted 'Commission on Pornography', whose use of that pejorative word set the tone and foresaw the conclusion of its 'report', included films in its overall purview.

In the eighteen months which followed, we talked to representatives of eleven organisations concerned with film censorship and four other individuals who were or had been actively involved with it. The British Board of Film Censors and the two film trade bodies which represented distributors and exhibitors were obvious choices and we added to them the two trades unions representing respectively the cinema staffs and the actors, as well as the British Film Institute which was concerned with film as an art. The organs of law and government were represented by the Metropolitan Police, the Home Office and the Association of Metropolitan Authorities. The Church of England Board of Social Responsibility spoke for the established

[1] Guy Phelps' study, *Film Censorship* (Gollancz) was not published until late in 1975.

church and the London Baptist Association submitted their views without being asked. Pressure groups on either side were the Festival of Light and the much smaller group of film buffs formed by a journalist, David Godin, into the Campaign for the Abolition of Film Censorship for Adults. We met the two London film critics, Felix Barker and Alexander Walker, and the solicitor John Montgomerie who had been Chairman of the Arts Council Inquiry into the obscenity laws. Last but not least we saw the former Secretary to the British Board of Film Censors, John Trevelyan.

John Trevelyan was in the curious position of game-keeper turned poacher. As chief censor in the 1960s he had been responsible for 'liberalizing' the practice of censorship. He had raised the age for the exclusion of children from adult films from 16 to 18 in the hope that it would eventually be possible to free adult films entirely from censorship. Trevelyan had an unrivalled knowledge of the film world, from the truly creative film makers to the more commercially motivated, and had come to the conclusion after thirteen years in the job that censorship for adults should go. Trevelyan's view was also held by the film critic, Alexander Walker of the Evening Standard and at that stage (although he later reneged) by Felix Barker of the Evening News, by the Campaign for the Abolition of Film Censorship for Adults, and by the actors' union Equity, who were opposed to censorship in all the arts.

The case for continuing prior censorship was put by the then Secretary of the British Board of Film Censors, Stephen Murphy, by the Home Office, the Church of England Board of Social Responsibility and the Festival of Light. Murphy based his case on the control of the violence content in films, which he felt to be harmful, rather than on the sex content, where he saw the Board's role as defining the limits of public acceptability and taste. The Home Office view was that the present system worked reasonably well and should be continued. Prior censorship enabled films to be stopped before commercial exploitation could occur and local authority licensing allowed an element of local discretion. The Church of England Board of Social Responsibility based the case for continued censorship on the need to protect the emotionally immature and to enable individuals to mature without undue exposure to scenes of callousness and violence on the screen. The London Baptist Association commented that films could adversely affect social attitudes by portraying as normal and acceptable behaviour which until recently was thought unacceptable.

An interesting viewpoint was put by the solicitor John Montgomerie on the respective merits of prior censorship and legal control. He opposed prior censorship and thought that the Theatres Act of 1968, which abolished prior censorship in the theatre, had had beneficial effects. Montgomerie had acted as Chairman of the Arts Council Inquiry into the obscenity laws which had concluded that they should be abolished in relation to adults. He pointed out that the present law on obscenity, notably the Obscene Publications Act of 1959 on which the Theatres Act was based, created many problems of interpretation in its own right for juries. The definition of obscenity in the Acts was where the effect of the material, if 'taken as a whole', was such as to tend to 'deprave and corrupt' persons likely to read, see or hear it. The definition was itself subject to numerous interpretations and could mean that which causes the recipient to become sexually excited. It was therefore an offence to cause others to become sexually excited, although that feeling in itself was no offence. He also commented that a local authority film licensing committee was about as suitable as a jury for making judgements on obscenity in films.

The comments of the Metropolitan Police representatives about the stimulus effect of violence in films on behaviour was one of scepticism. They said that they found more trouble with audiences after rock beat films had been shown than after films in which violence was depicted and thought that peculiar people were to be found in any cinema, regardless of the film shown.

Both the film trade representatives stressed the usefulness of film censorship to them in allowing for careful planning of programmes on their circuits over a period, and in protecting them from prosecution in the courts. They also emphasised the casual nature of much cinema going and the wide social spectrum of the audiences which in their view required some degree of control on the acceptability of the films shown. The British Film Institute felt unable, as a government funded institution, to express any opinion on censorship of the medium of which it was the artistic custodian. The National Association of Theatrical and Kinematograph Employees (NATKE) had no union view on censorship.

While the exercise of meeting the different organisations was useful to us in sounding out opinion, it provided no surprises. It told us what we had already suspected, that the trade, the BBFC, the Church, and the Home Office liked the system, while the film critics, the actors' union, and the former chief censor did not.

The second part of our enquiry was into public attitudes towards film censorship. We decided that the only way to carry this out was by commissioning an attitudes survey by a professional firm. Among the firms which tendered, we chose the one which rejected a simple series of questions of the 'do you like film censorship?' variety in favour of a greater probing of attitudes in depth. We had become increasingly aware that attitudes towards film censorship were complicated and often contradictory: some people would, for example, emphatically say that they opposed censorship but then qualify their statement by expressing the view that a particular film should have been banned. Sometimes they appeared to respond in what they felt was the correct stance from a sociopolitical viewpoint, whether of 'liberalism' or 'maintaining standards', but at other times their response might be their own degree of reticence in matters concerning sexuality and their feelings of aggression and sexual drive.

The survey organisation that we approached decided to do an exploratory study on attitudes to film censorship before making recommendations for a full scale study. They carried out four group discussions with separate groups of men and women, one each of a younger and older age group of both working and middle class and also tried out a structured interview on a small sample group. Their report[1] showed clearly the complexity and inconsistency of people's responses. First, the system of censorship was complicated and not always easy to understand with the number of different bodies involved. Then, the replies to general statements on censorship and on specific themes differed greatly. Even the questions on whether murder or rape should be shown in films proved difficult to answer because of the varying treatment in different films and the context of particular scenes. Murder in a conventional western movie for example would have a very different effect on the viewer than, say, the murder shown in Hitchcock's *Psycho*.

The researchers were however able to identify four different types of respondents in the population. These they described as:

1. Pro-censorship censors who believe in censorship and even want it increased. Their answer to detailed questions about particular types of scenes remained consistent in wanting to ban or cut them.
2. Anti-censorship censors who were against censorship in principle but, in considering particular scenes, were quite prepared to suggest that many should be cut or banned.
3. Pro-censorship non-censors who believed in censorship in principle but were unable to suggest scenes which

[1] R. Jowell, J. Spence, G. Shaheen, 'Film Censorship Exploratory Study', Social and Community Planning Research, 1974.

43

should actually be cut out or banned.

4. Anti-censorship non-censors who were against censorship both in principle and in practice.

The report recommended the Council to join with the Home Office and the British Board of Film Censors in sponsoring a national survey which 'could be extremely informative not only about film censorship but about the whole question of freedom and protection. It would touch heavily on the current debate on laws about pornography; it would discover more about attitudes towards permissiveness, etc., and it would throw valuable light on the conflicts and concerns within the population about the taboos which are increasingly becoming non-taboos.'

The Council's Film Viewing Board accepted the report and approached the British Board of Film Censors and the Home Office for support for a national survey, but both turned us down. Although they both spoke of the difficulties in assessing opinion on such a complex subject, neither were prepared to join in a survey which would attempt to overcome them. Their refusals were consistent with the overall attitudes of the Home Office and BBFC which were that the system as it stood worked, and that if it was in danger of falling down, all efforts should be directed to shoring it up. In such a context, an inquiry into anything so basic as the attitudes towards film censorship of those being censored was clearly thought to be unnecessary.

The refusal of the Home Office and the BBFC to join in a survey meant that we were unable to go ahead. The cost of continuing on our own was disproportionately high and the Council in 1974 was beginning to cut back on expenditure which was felt to be inessential. It was a lost opportunity which I very much regretted.

In our final report we were, however, able to draw on some other surveys on allied subjects. One on indecency, chiefly referring to public display, was published in a Sunday newspaper.[1] In one answer to a question as to

[1] *Sunday Times*, 30/12/73.

whether the respondent had been 'seriously upset' by something indecent shown in a film, only 8%, said that they had (5% of men and 10% of women) compared with 14% who had been upset by a TV play. Such a low response might, however, have reflected the low incidence of cinema going compared with TV viewing. An earlier survey on 'permissiveness'[1] found that 56% of the respondents favoured the free availability of pornographic books and magazines provided they were not publicly displayed, and 52 % found that the moral climate was about right. Both surveys showed women as more likely to be shocked than men.

The third part of our enquiry was to assess the research findings on the influence of films on behaviour. So much was made in the newspapers of the baneful effects of film that we hoped that a cool look at the basic research would be helpful. We found that the number of studies on violence which had been made was considerable, a clear reflection of the public's continuing concern particularly in relation to children. For example, UNESCO had carried out two projects in 1961 and 1964 on the influence of cinema and TV respectively on children and adolescents. In the U.S.A., major reports had been published by the National Commission on the Causes and Prevention of Violence on *Violence and the Media* in 1969, and by the Surgeon-General's Scientific Advisory Committee on Television and Social Behaviour on *Television and Growing up: the impact of televised violence* in 1972. In Britain, a Leicester University study on *Television and Delinquency* appeared in 1970. The general conclusion of these studies and reports was that violence in film and television was not a prime cause of violent behaviour, although it might trigger off violence in a small number of disturbed individuals. The roots of violence lay deep in emotional, family, and social situations, and the media played a very minor role. The long term effects of continual exposure to filmed violence were

[1] *Sunday Times*, 25/2/73.

harder to assess, and the possibility of accustoming viewers to aggressive behaviour in a justifiable cause might unduly influence people in favour of violence.

The evidence on sexual material was less prolific. In Britain there had been an enquiry into the obscenity laws set up by the Chairman of the Arts Council whose findings, published in 1969, included an assessment of experience in Denmark and the opinion of a consultant psychiatrist. The report by the Longford Committee investigating Pornography (1972) had included an assessment of relevant research by a psychologist, Maurice Yaffe which failed to provide the Longford Committee with the evidence they would have liked. But the major research study published in 1970 and running to some twelve volumes of empirical study and evidence was the report of the American Commission on Obscenity and Pornography.

The American Commission had a chequered career. It was appointed by President Johnson in 1967 and included many eminent academics. When President Nixon came to office in 1968 he hastily appointed to it a further nominee, one Charles Keating. Mr Keating, founder of an organisation called Citizens for Decent Literature, took no part in the Commission's discussions. He nevertheless produced a minority report to the Commission's main report which attacked the 'preconceived conclusions of the Commission majority who are dedicated to a position of complete moral anarchy'[1] and asserted that 'One can consult all the experts he chooses, can write reports, make studies etc. but the fact that obscenity corrupts lies within the common sense, the reason and the logic of every man.'[2] Mr Keating was joined by two other dissentients and with their minority reports to help him, President Nixon was able to say of the Commission's findings 'I have evaluated that report and categorically reject its morally bankrupt conclusions and major

[1] *Report of the Commission on Obscenity and Pornography*, U.S. Government Printing Office, 1970, p. 537.
[2] Ibid., p. 544.

recommendations. So long as I am in the White House, there will be no relaxation of the national effort to control and eliminate smut from our national life ... American morality is not to be trifled with.'[1] The conclusions which Nixon was at such pains to reject were that sight of pornographic materials had little or no effect on sexuality or sexual morality and played no significant role in causing delinquent or criminal behaviour. The Commission therefore recommended that such materials should be freely available to adults, though not to children, and that the obscenity laws should be repealed. A massive sex education programme should be launched, its purpose 'to contribute to healthy attitudes and orientations to sexual relationships'.[2] Perhaps the most striking sentence in the report and the strongest contrast to Mr Nixon's use of the term 'smut' is the assertion that 'The Commission believes that interest in sex is normal, healthy, good.'[3] Needless to say, no action was taken by the federal government on any of the Commission's recommendations in America.

Three further sections of our report dealt with the law relating to film censorship, cinema advertising, and the enforcement of age limits. On the legal provisions affecting films, we reported that neither a British Board of Film Censors certificate nor a local authority licence such as might be granted by the GLC protected a film from legal prosecution. There were a number of laws and provisions of the common law, some dating from earlier statutes and framed for other purposes than films, which could be used against them. The list comprised the Customs Consolidation Act of 1876 which allowed customs officers to seize indecent or obscene articles, the Post Office Act which allowed the seizure of indecent material sent through the post, the Race Relations Act in relation to films alleged to incite race hatred, the common law with respect to

[1] *The Obscenity Report*, Olympia Press, 1971, pp. 33 and 35.
[2] *Report of the Commission on Obscenity and Pornography*, op. cit., p. 48.
[3] Ibid., p. 47.

outraging public decency, the publication of an obscene libel, keeping a 'disorderly house' (and therein holding exhibitions outraging public decency), and conspiring to corrupt public morals.

During the course of the two years when I was Chairman of the Film Viewing Board, five attempts were made by the anti-pornography 'crusaders' to invoke one or other of these legal provisions. The first of these was an action against *Blow Out* brought by Mary Whitehouse under the section of the Vagrancy Acts 1824 and 1836 which made it an offence to hold an indecent exhibition in a public place. The action was not successful because the magistrate held that a cinema was not a public place within the meaning of the Act. The second was a prosecution initiated by Edward Shackleton against the distributors of *Last Tango* under the section of the Obscene Publications Act relating to the distribution and storing of obscene material. Again it was unsuccessful because the High Court ruled that as the Act expressly excluded the exhibition of films from its provisions, an action against the distributors did not make sense as the holding of a film could not be said to 'deprave and corrupt' the distributor.

Two actions were brought against the film *Deep Throat* which was never submitted to the British Board of Film Censors for certification. The first involved the GLC. The Film Viewing Board had been asked by the National Co-ordinating Committee against Censorship, who wanted to hold a one day seminar on film censorship, to waive its censorship requirements for the occasion so that parts of *Deep Throat* and other uncertificated film clips could be shown to an invited audience. The Board agreed unanimously after hearing that speakers from all sides would be invited to join the discussions, and that invitations had gone out to Lord Longford and Mary Whitehouse. What then happened was a good example of the usual Longford-Whitehouse tactics of applying pressure in all possible quarters. The seminar organisers were informed that the Customs and Excise department would refuse the importation of *Deep Throat* as an indecent article. Such action effectively negated the licensing powers of the GLC and we therefore, invited a representative of the Customs department to explain his position. The Customs Officer pointed out that his department's powers existed independently of our Council's and said that he had had numerous pressing phone calls from Mary Whitehouse, who knew of the seminar because she had been invited to take part in it, urging him to ban the importation of the film. He and his fellow officers had viewed a print and could not avoid concluding that it was indecent, and had therefore advised the distributor Jimmy Vaughan that it would be seized if brought into the country. Vaughan could, had he wished, have appealed against the Customs decision, and a case would have had to go to the Courts for decision. Vaughan had, however, himself said on several occasions that the film was indecent but that he saw no need on those grounds to ban it and possibly felt that he was on poor ground for an appeal against a verdict of 'indecency'. There was a sequel to this curious tale. Although *Deep Throat* was officially not permitted to enter Britain, it had in fact been circulating unofficially at private film shows and clubs for some time. An action was brought against a network of North London clubs showing *Deep Throat* and other films under the charge of keeping a 'disorderly house' and screening indecent films therein. The all-male jury decided to acquit, much to everyone's surprise.[1]

The last legal action brought was far reaching in its consequences. The council's Film Viewing Board passed the Swedish sex education film *More About the Language of Love*, a sequel to *The Language of Love* which the GLC passed in 1970 and which the British Board of Film Censors had eventually certificated. The film contained one purple passage which showed actual intercourse between a man and woman. Raymond Blackburn and Lord Longford complained about the film and the Director of Public

[1] *The Guardian*, 25/6/74.

Prosecutions seized it in July 1974 and initiated a prosecution under the common law provision forbidding an indecent exhibition. When the case came to trial, defending counsel argued that the case should be dismissed because the common law in question was meant to apply to public places but never to cinemas at which people had to pay to gain admittance. Judge Gwyn Morris however was not sympathetic to this viewpoint. He argued that a person seeking shelter from the rain might choose to pay for a ticket to a cinema in order to save himself from the deluge and thus be exposed to an indecent exhibition unwittingly. With this extraordinary but ingenious justification, his ruling was that the common law on indecency did apply to films in licensed cinemas and meant that the trial could proceed. The jury, which under the common law was not allowed to hear expert testimony of any kind, found the charge proven and the verdict guilty. The verdict was a good illustration of the vagaries of the jury system. Almost a year earlier, *Deep Throat*, a film admittedly pornographic in intent, was not found indecent while *More About the Language of Love* was. While both films contained material of oral/genital contact, *More About* ... had only brief shots shown as part of the lovemaking prior to intercourse while *Deep Throat* purports to be a celebration of oral sex. The success of the action against *More About* ... encouraged Raymond Blackburn to bring an action against the Greater London Council requiring the Council to amend its terms of management on film censorship to conform with the common law. Blackburn and his friends knew that the Council's terms of management, adopted in 1965, were based on the provisions of the Obscene Publications Act. The Council was required to judge whether a film was likely to 'deprave and corrupt' and not whether it was indecent. Blackburn's action, which went before the High Court and then the Court of Appeal was eventually successful, and the Council had to amend its terms of management in May 1976 to include films which 'outraged the standards of public decency'. This episode was an undoubted success in forcing a return, at least on paper, to the older, looser definition of indecency and away from the definition which judged films on the same criteria as books and plays.

Cinema publicity advertising had long caused concern to the Council and was the subject of more complaints from the public than the actual films. There has always been a tendency for films to be advertised in terms of superlative adjectives and claims to shock, horrify, or amaze. Managers like to put these 'come on' slogans outside their cinemas and to add to them photographs from the films or, better still, blown up photos of scantily clad females. The film trade itself attempts to control poster, press, and front of house advertising through its Advertisement Viewing Committee, which includes representatives of the Kinematograph Renters' Society, the poster advertising industry, the newspaper industry, British Transport Advertising Ltd and London Transport. Advertisements are vetted by the Committee, but not all cinemas co-operate with it. In 1971, the GLC had considered making the vetting of advertisements by the Committee compulsory as part of the terms of its licence but agreed not to do so provided the Advertisement Viewing Committee could secure greater conformity to its rulings. The Council exercises its authority under its licensing powers to prohibit publicity unsuitable for general exhibition only in the case of films given an 'X' London certificate. In those cases, front of house publicity and visual material are vetted by GLC officers.

In 1973, the Cinematograph and Indecent Displays Bill had set out to make indecent public display an offence at law. The Bill fell with the Conservative Government and was not reintroduced because of the many pitfalls revealed in it at the Committee stage, but there was general concern on the question of display expressed by MPs of all parties. Although not a case for a criminal prosecution, there appeared to me to be a case for controlling the display of material which offended people and which they could not avoid when walking in the street, which posed a very different problem to material which was deliberately sought out as entertainment. The GLC's control of front of house publicity of 'X' London films fell within this category.

A further problem concerned the person who visits a cinema casually and may be misled by the title as to its contents. During the course of our interviews with interested organisations, we had been given some amusing examples. The coach load of Women's Institute ladies visited the hip cartoon *Fritz the Cat* on the mistaken assumption that they were going to see *Felix the Cat* or some other Disney product. Another was *The Boys in the Band*, a story of homosexuality, to which one of our interviewees took his elderly mother thinking that it was a musical. If there was never a visitor to *Last Tango* who thought it was about ballroom dancing, that might only be because the film had received such wide and notorious publicity.

It seemed to me that there was a case for more information in cinemas to acquaint the public with the content of films. In 1973 I therefore proposed that the Film Viewing Board should adopt several possible measures to ensure a more informative service to cinema patrons. One proposal was a requirement that the title of the film should give a clear indication of its theme. Another was that a brief factual description of the film should be clearly displayed in the cinema foyer. The third proposal was to place warning notices in the foyer advising patrons that a film contained material which some might find offensive. The Board decided to adopt these procedures on an experimental basis in spite of some misgivings as to whether it was going to be possible to write plot descriptions that were accurate and helpful, but which did not either give away the film's plot or act as a sensational 'come on'.

We first tried this new policy in the case of *Blow Out*. We

52

asked the film distributors to write a two line description of the film which we vetted for accuracy and lack of sensationalism. After several efforts, it eventually read 'A black comedy about four world weary pleasure seekers who decide to eat themselves to death in an orgy of high cuisine and sexual indulgence.' To this we added a larger notice that 'The Greater London Council advises that this film contains material which may offend some people' and above that, the film's title, its certificate ('X' London) and in large letters on top the legend 'IMPORTANT NOTICE'. The whole was written on a placard and placed next to the cinema box office inside the foyer. Our reports from the cinema staff indicated that the public appreciated the information and there were no objections to it. The success of this little venture was, however overshadowed by press controversy following Mary Whitehouse's staged 'walk out'. From this I learned one important lesson, that the anti-pornography 'crusaders' had no desire to be forewarned and protected from unintentional offence. They simply wanted films which they found offensive banned to everyone else. In our review of film censorship we were, however, told that the cinema exhibitors thought our move was a helpful one. GLC inspectors who made enquiries estimated that about one third of cinema patrons read the notices, and reported one case of a patron who, after reading the notice, decided not to see the film. We therefore continued to use one or a combination of the three policies in the case of several films awarded an 'X' London certificate when the occasion warranted it.

A further aspect of our enquiry was into the enforcement of age limits when admission to 'X' films was sought. We found that both cinema managers and staff representatives were aware of their obligation to refuse admission to the under eighteens and tried to carry it out conscientiously. They were, however, in a very real difficulty since the actual age of youngsters in thear late teens is hard to distinguish. Differing individual rates of maturity meant that one youngster could easily be taken for 18 when she was 14, while another could not. It was an inevitable problem if the estimation of age was made on appearance alone. The only other way of enforcing the regulation would be to require young people to carry identification which would give their date of birth. One of the strongest arguments put to us against the end of censorship for adults was that teenagers do frequently succeed in getting into cinemas showing 'X' films. If there was no censorship for adults, teenagers were likely to see highly pornographic material thought to be unsuitable for them. These fears are widespread and reflect the concern of parents for their growing children and perhaps also the way parents project their own uncertainties and concerns onto their youngsters. If genuine feelings were to be assuaged, it would be necessary to require identification to be provided. We considered but rejected the possibility of cinemas issuing identity cards showing age because of a general feeling amongst us against such papers. But if they are the key to a privilege, they may be accepted more readily than we thought at the time. Old age pensioners' bus passes, for example, are highly acceptable.

Finally, we rounded off our enquiry with some investigation of film censorship in other countries. Of the countries from which we were able to get information, we found that Australia had the strictest censorship, which extended to books as well as to films. The Australian Federal Goverment has a Board of Censors operating within its Customs department. France, too, has a Minister responsible for censorship which is carried out by a Control Commission underneath the Minister. More recently, however, since Giscard d'Estaing has been President, there has been a relaxation of censorship with regard to sex films, although an extra tax has been imposed on their exhibition. France's neighbour, Belgium, has no censorship for adults and a special commission to approve films for those under 16 years. Films are, however, subject to criminal law prohibiting shows judged to be contrary to public morality. Denmark has no film censorship for adults and has gone further by abolishing its obscenity laws, except for exhibition in public places. In the U.S.A. obscenity is the only lawful ground for censorship. Prior censorship has been abolished, but legal actions may be brought against films and film classification remains. Our enquiries thus showed that Britain continued to exercise the most severe form of film censorship of any democratic country we looked at, with the exception of Australia.

4

REPORTING TO THE COUNCIL

By the autumn of 1974 our enquiries into the law and practice of film censorship in London and on the effects of films on behaviour had been completed. It was time to draw up a report for the Film Viewing Board on our investigations and to decide on our recommendations.

The opinions which we had canvassed provided no surprises. There was a difference of opinion on the usefulness of censorship between the various organisations and people involved with films, with the weight of the Home Office, the film trade organisations[1], and the Church put behind continuing censorship. The public's attitude towards being censored, from our limited surveys, indicated a complex set of responses to both the idea and the practice of censorship in particular cases. Our assessment of the research evidence gave no support to the view that films were the cause of delinquency and violent behaviour. It was evident that the law relating to film censorship was very disorganised and in need of clarification, although certain legal powers to control film content did exist. It was also clear that Britain had one of the strictest systems of film censorship of the countries in Western Europe and the English speaking world. My own assessment was that our system was bolstered by paternalistic habit and irrational fear rather than by positive evidence of a need for control.

The options open to us were to present the report with no recommendations for a major change in the system, to recommend a change and instruct that our views be

[1] The organisations changed their view in 1975, and have since advocated the withdrawal of local authority powers to censor films for adult audiences.

forwarded to the Home Office, or to recommend and actually carry out a change within the powers we had. If we were convinced that prior censorship for adults should be brought to an end, the first course of action was wrong. The second possibility, making recommendations to the Home Office, did not offer much hope. The Home Office had already twice turned down pleas from the previous Council for an enquiry, and had recently refused to join us in a survey of public attitudes towards censorship. It seemed doubtful that further representations would stir them to action. They were more likely to argue that London's views should not be taken as representing the whole nation's and instruct us to soldier on. That left us with the third possibility, to act on our opinion. The powers given to local authorities to censor films were mandatory regarding children under 16, but permissive for those over 16. We were not obliged to censor films for adults and could pass a simple resolution in Council at any time resolving not to exercise our powers. The results of our action would be striking. Because British Board of Film Censors certificates could only be enforced through local authority licensing powers, our resolution to end the exercise of those powers would mean that a film could be shown if it had not got an 'X' certificate, or could be shown unmarked by the cuts that the BBFC had insisted on as a price of that certificate. Moreover, since London contained a seventh of all the cinemas in the country, we would be punching a huge hole in the national system of film censorship. The Home Office would then be stirred from its stodgy inertia to consider that system seriously and from the foundations up. The fine tuning and tinkering so beloved of civil servants would have to be pushed aside in the face of the massive challenge which we would pose. We could then expect to see a quick flurry of consultations at the top which might hopefully end in a reform of the law which would put films in cinemas on the same legal basis as books and the theatre, as we had urged.

On the opposite side of the argument were the possibilities that we would lose the vote in Council and return to the status quo, that success would create chaos and uncertainty for the film trade, or that we might provoke a 'backlash' from the Government and Parliament. Of these objections, the second was certainly true, but fears on the part of the film trade would lead to pressure on the Home Office for change and that was what we wanted. As for the backlash, it was already apparent in the active role played by the Director of Public Prosecutions in bringing a charge against *More About the Language of Love*, a film which we had licensed. If the DPP was ready to prosecute films we had licensed, where was the much vaunted local option that the Home Office was always telling us about? It appeared to exist only to allow local authorities to be more repressive than the British Board of Film Censors. The Home Office on the other hand, was politically headed by Roy Jenkins who had been responsible as a private member for the Obscene Publications Act in 1959. There was a good chance that he would favour the extension of that Act's provisions to films. My own assessment was that it was worth pushing ahead with the recommendations. At worst, we would have put our views fairly and squarely on the record for the consideration of our colleagues and the public, and initiated a debate on the justice and merits of the system. At best, we would succeed in abolishing censorship for adults in the Greater London area and would start a process which might well be copied by other local authorities and lead to a national reform of film censorship. It was within our power as a Council to pull the rug out from under the system, and that was well worth doing.

I therefore drafted a private memorandum for my Labour colleagues on the Film Viewing Board recommending that the Council cease to exercise its powers to censor films for adults over the age of 18 with the effect that any film which did not fall foul of the law could be shown in London's cinemas. The recommendations were accepted and passed to a meeting of the entire majority Labour group. It was clear from the discussion there that a big majority of the Labour Councillors favoured the change. The problem was not, therefore, to win a majority, but to see how big a minority were opposed to it. Traditionally, film viewing had not been regarded as a party issue. Judgements on individual films were never made on a party basis and the issue of censorship was regarded by many as a 'conscience' matter. The opponents to our recommendations put the case for a 'conscience' decision strongly, arguing that there should be a free vote not subject to the Whips in the Council. Our view was that a decision not to exercise any of the Council's powers was clearly a major question of policy which should be decided by the majority group as other major policy questions were. Recognising the force of the 'conscience' argument, we recommended that those with a strong conscience view against should be entitled to abstain. The argument in the majority group centred on this issue, rather than on the merits of the proposal, and the vote went very narrowly in favour of allowing a 'free' vote in the Council chamber. Many of those in favour of giving up censorship argued that consistency demanded that a plea for people to make up their own minds about films required a demonstration of that principle in the Council Chamber on the decision of whether or not to censor. I certainly appreciated that argument but also realised that a 'free' vote strengthened the chances of defeat enormously. It was not clear what support we would get from the Conservatives and the two Liberals, but it might well not cancel out the number of negative votes from Labour Councillors.

Once the decision was taken to present the Film Viewing Board's recommendations to the Council, we had to draft a report. The Council's officers drafted the account of our investigations but declined to put out recommendations. When a matter was highly contentious and not clearly susceptible to professional, dispassionate advice, it was not unusual for the officers to request the Chairman of the relevant committee to draft the recommendations. I therefore wrote a separate paper which summarised the enquiry as I saw it and argued for reform, recommending that the Council cease to exercise its powers to censor films for adults over 18 years old and that arrangements for controlling cinema advertising and providing adequate information about films in cinema foyers should be reviewed. The nub of the argument was that the onus was on the censors to justify continuing our option for prior censorship.

'The burden of justification for the continued exercise of that option has not been made. That being so, the right of individual adults to decide their own choice of films must remain paramount, and corresponds to the freedom to read uncensored books and see uncensored plays. If adults in a free society are deemed fit to vote and decide the Government of the day, or in time of war may die in defence of their country and the values of freedom and democracy, it is consistent that they should also as adults have the freedom to view the films they wish, subject only to the laws enacted by Parliament. The Council should not be the agent of an enforced morality; each man or woman should have the right to determine their own moral code.'[1]

Once the reports had been prepared they could be made available to the public and I therefore decided to hold a press conference in order to launch them. We no longer had the advantage of issuing straight news as my earlier document sent to Labour colleagues had been leaked to the *Daily Telegraph*.[2] The knowledge that it must have been one of my Labour councillor colleagues who had done so was no comfort at all. The *Daily Telegraph* disclosure was followed by comment and letters of a familiar kind. Mary Whitehouse demanded to know the source of our research showing the lack of connection between pornography and crime and, when referred to the U.S. Commission Report on Obscenity and Pornography, came back with an attempt to discredit the evidence presented by accusing the

[1]GLC Committee Paper 'The Future of Film Censorship for Adults'.
[2]*Daily Telegraph* 12/11/74

Commission of suppressing allegedly valid evidence proving the opposite.[1] The Telegraph's columnist clutched at the straw of instinct and commonsense, very much as Mr Keating, Nixon's appointee, did in writing his minority report to the U.S. Commission's Report. In *Way of the World*, the Telegraph man described the Commission's conclusions as 'sophistry': ' ... the idea that unless something can be scientifically proved to be wrong or harmful, even though every normal human instinct and every normal instinct of commonsense tells us that it is wrong and harmful then it cannot be so.'[2] The absurdity of this kind of argument can be seen if, say, witchcraft is substituted for pornography. Five hundred years ago 'every normal human instinct' affirmed the existence of witches who exerted evil influence and ought therefore to be tortured and killed. Only 40 years ago the 'normal instinct of commonsense' of most Germans knew that Aryans were a superior race. If for 'normal instinct' is substituted 'my own personal prejudices', and for 'commonsense' 'my refusal to read and consider dispassionate evidence and to modify my prejudices accordingly', the Telegraph columnist's outpouring reads more accurately.

Our press conference passed off without incident and the reporting of it was straightforward and fair. Comment was limited, almost as if the editorial staff were not quite sure what their attitudes should be. Alexander Walker, film critic of the *Evening Standard*, made the fullest and most favourable analysis of the likely effect of our proposed action and gave us warm support.[3] Felix Barker, the *Evening News* film critic, regurgitated the BBFC line that the GLC as a 'liberal' appeal body better ensured the showing of controversial films than a completely open situation would do since the cinema exhibitors would be fearful of prosecutions. He added, 'This curious arrange-

[1] Ibid., 16/11/74, 23/11/74, 2/12/74.
[2] Ibid., 13/11/74.
[3] *Evening Standard*, 5/12/74.

ment may seem hypocritical, but it is a typically enlightened English way of getting round a tricky situation.'[1] Quite. To paraphrase: We English are delightfully hypocritical and irrational but, in our wholly charming and wise way, we have produced a chewing gum and string solution which works (or should work if everyone sensible co-operated to make it work). Only the *News of the World* came smartly out with a strong condemnation of our proposal which ended 'God preserve us from the freedom fighters. If they have their way, we shall end up with no freedom at all.'[2] The media judged the subject to be of world wide interest. Friends in America and Australia wrote to tell me that they had seen reports in their local press or heard radio comments. Another friend sent me a clipping from the English language *Bangkok Post* (with the cheerful comment 'World Fame at last!') and I wondered what on earth the people in Thailand found to interest them in London's screen proposals.

More to the point, the cinema trade journal ran an account of our plans with contributions from different people in the business. Protection of the trade featured prominently in their viewpoint and they feared the uncertainty which would result from our action. *Cinema and TV Today* reported that 'There are fears in the film industry that abolition of censorship for the over-18s may lead to total anarchy around the country. Each local licensing authority may want to censor films according to its own ideas.'[3] The Secretary of the Cinema Exhibitors' Association said 'Obviously, we are going to be in terrible trouble if we never know whether a film is going to be all right until it is prosecuted ... If the GLC starts to cease to exercise their rights of censorship they are leaving a vacuum which Parliament has not yet filled.'[4] The Chair-

[1] *Evening News*, 6/12/74.
[2] *News of the World*, 8/12/74.
[3] *Cinema & TV Today*, 4/1/75.
[4] Ibid.

man of the Kinematograph Manufacturers' Association feared that 'if you are going to cut it [censorship] all out the floodgates will be opened and if Mrs Wistrich gets her way, the lawyers will be rubbing their hands with glee because it is going to be open season for cinema owners who are prepared to accept the risk of being taken to court'.[1] Columnist David Lewin, however, argued that 'It is time the film industry grew up and accepted its responsibilities for itself and what it does, without having a shield ... In the end the industry will be better for having to accept the responsibility, legal and otherwise, when a film runs into trouble. It should no longer shelter behind a censorship shield which everyone knows to be its own creation.'[2] Former censor John Trevelyan said 'I am broadly in favour of the [GLC] viewing board's recommendation. My point is that it is a question of self responsibility. If the industry puts on a film that runs into trouble, then it should take individual responsibility.'[3] Director Michael Winner thought that the fears of the trade were exaggerated. Referring to the U.S.A. he said that 'A few test cases have come up in the courts there but these have not interrupted the normal distribution of motion pictures, and nor are they likely to over here. I would certainly rather a jury ultimately decided, in a few test cases, what was considered by the community palatable for an audience of the day, than have the ludicrous arguments of the 'cut one stabbing and we'll give it an "X"' type thing that goes on in the censor's office at the moment. The British Board of Film Censors has not stopped test cases being brought in the courts here anyway.'[4]

As the time drew near for the debate and vote in Council, lobbying began in earnest. The film trade weighed in with a powerful argument for the status quo.

[1] Ibid., 11/1/75.
[2] Ibid.
[3] Ibid.
[4] *Cinema & TV Today*, 25/1/75.

Signed by the Presidents of the Cinematograph Exhibitors' Association, Kinematograph Renters' Society, and Association of Independent Cinemas, the letter argued that in the absence of the application of the Obscene Publications Act to films, the removal of the local licensing power to censor films for adults would lead to a resort to common law. 'We fear that the cinema will become a target of the common informer or of private prosecutions by persons or institutions whose views may not coincide with current public taste. The only defence available in a prosecution at common law is that the film itself does not offend ... The film is therefore more vulnerable and more open to attack than books and other publications or theatrical productions which are now respectively covered by the Obscene Publications Act 1959 and the Theatres Act 1968 ... We anticipate that the effect of the abandonment of the exercise of the GLC's control will be twofold: first, that a number of cinemas will take the risk of showing obscene material and, secondly, that most distributors and exhibitors will adopt a cautious attitude – there being no yardstick on which they can rely.' The trade then ended by deploring our proposal to give up 'responsibilities which Parliament assumed would continue to be exercised by local authorities ... In our opinion, such a sweeping change should not be made in the absence of new legislation affecting the whole country.' This letter, which was circulated to all Councillors on the decision of the Council's officers, was an influential contribution against our recommendations because it pointed out the weakness in the existing law and suggested that it was irresponsible for the Council to proceed without the agreement of the trade and, indeed, of Parliament. It was likely to influence adversely the senior members of the Council who preferred to move forward on the basis of an agreed consensus and to avoid controversy other than the orthodox party political debate.

The trade's contribution was however measured and moderate compared to letters protesting against our proposals which now began to come to every Councillor. Although a few were reasoned, others were abusive and some violent and hysterical. Many expressed a religious conviction as a basis for their objections. Others professed a concern for moral corruption and for the care of the young. It seemed that some correspondents saw in our action an overthrow of all responsibility, morality and stability in society in favour of anarchy, lust and hate. I do not know to what extent they were prompted by the organisations of the pro-censorship lobby. Certainly those organisations were active, and several circulated letters and memoranda to Councillors. The Nationwide Festival of Light for example argued that 'The state of contemporary society cried out for restraint' and that 'Central and local government have a duty to protect ordinary citizens from exploitation and corruption'. Mr J.H. Court, a lecturer in psychology at Flinders University, South Australia and a member of the Australian Festival of Light, sent an open letter to all GLC members alleging that only since the publication of the American Commission Report on Obscenity and Pornography had evidence become convincing that social harm resulted from sex films. 'I therefore ask that you give serious attention to the strong probability that a significant rise in serious offences even beyond the existing problems in the London area will occur if you remove all restraint. I believe the women and children of London are entitled to know that they especially will be placed in unnecessary danger from such a decision.' The Church of England Board of Social Responsibility also decided to enter the debate by making a statement to the press opposing the proposed GLC action. Although the Board accepted that individual freedoms should be safeguarded, 'it considers however that this must be set alongside the need for society to express its concern for standards which keep it healthy and vigorous, to teach its members what these standards are, and to protect its weaker members.'

The Board of Deputies of British Jews circulated a

letter expressing grave concern 'lest the abolition of the regulations which presently protect minority groups against incitement to racial hatred will open the floodgates of prejudice and animosity to the detriment of that communal harmony to which we all aspire'. Since the Race Relations Act applied to films as to all other media, the Board of Deputies' letter showed an unexpected lack of understanding of that law, but perhaps the real concern of the letter was expressed in the sentiment that 'the public must protect itself against the pernicious influence of films that debase the individual and undermine the moral foundations of society'.

The most singular contribution to these counter-letters and leaflets came from Mary Whitehouse in her capacity as Secretary of the National Viewers' and Listeners' Association. She chose to issue a pamphlet entitled 'Mrs Mary Whitehouse replies to Mrs Enid Wistrich' which consisted of a contrived dialogue between the two of us. Quotations from my paper to the Council were presented and carefully knocked down in replies from Mrs Whitehouse along predictable lines. Almost alone among the procensorship lobbyists she took the evidence on the effects of 'pornography' seriously enough to try to refute it on its own ground. She alleged for example that much of the evidence submitted to the U.S. Commission had been excluded from its consideration and that large numbers of psychiatrists and psychotherapists did think that there was a link between 'pornography' and sex crime. Mary Whitehouse also evidently saw me as a personal challenge to herself since she chose to personalise the issue between us. Her pamphlet and her subsequent appearance during the debate at County Hall indicated a desire not to be pushed out of the centre of the picture, which she had made so much her own, by any imagined rival in that role.

Another persistent opponent was David Holbrook who had engaged me in a long correspondence over the past year, and sent me a number of his books and articles. Holbrook saw 'pornography' as a debasement of love and an expression of hate, an immoral exploitation of sex by commercial interests. His descriptions of certain films which I had seen (and he usually had not) convinced me that, like many others, he built up great fantasies about films onto which he put his own strongly felt anxieties about the human condition. David Holbrook carried his views to the extreme of describing me in an article in the *Daily Mail* as 'one of the most dangerous women at large in Britain today'.[1] That particular article, however, resulted in about the nicest comment on the whole affair which I received. With a sublime disregard for David Holbrook's hysterical attack and an eye for realities, a lady from Basingstoke wrote to him, 'In your article about Mrs Wistrich in today's "Mail" you give a picture of her – I am really only interested in the jumper she is wearing and I want to find out if it's hand-knit and what pattern. I am an O.A.P. and not very interested in the views expressed – but if you would be kind enough to send this letter on to her, as you would know her address, I would be very grateful.' David Holbrook did so and it gave me a lot of pleasure amid all the morbid excitement to be able to give her the information required.

If the pensioner's letter was a pleasant relief, I also had to put up with a good deal of unpleasant and abusive correspondence which came from the allegedly religious. A Baptist minister wrote, 'After over 40 years in the Christian Ministry I have had some experience of human nature and have seen some of the ghastly disasters wrought by sexual perversities yet you, in your responsible position are apparently quite prepared to let any filthy film be shown ... Shame on you Mrs Wistrich – may God have mercy on you if you do not mend your ways.'

The displeasure of the religious was ecumenical – for good measure, I was told by a friend that I had been denounced from the pulpit of a local synagogue, and a Catholic priest personally told me of his own disgust at the

[1]*Daily Mail*, 28/1/75.

course I was following. Even these views were mild compared with some anonymous ones I received by letter. 'No wonder the world is degenerating while sex warped minded bitches like you are about. God's curse be upon you and your family' wrote one pure minded man.

Not all the correspondence I received was unpleasant. A smaller number of letters arraved in support of our stand and some were heartening. One gentleman of 70 wrote to me from Halifax, 'I am a churchman and keenly interested in social conditions as well as being deeply committed to socialism. The right to chose for myself is not something I will delegate to anyone willingly. If example is shown in the family and children know what is good and what is bad, they too will be able to select for themselves ... I have never been in agreement with the postulation that pornography is evil and a dangerous temptation for people to embark on an orgy of 'sinful' living.'

From the other end of the political spectrum, another said 'I am very, very English, a Tory, in fact a True Blue Tory, so I am sure you can understand how very much it hurts me to have to appeal to you a Socialist ... to fight for any aspect of freedom ... In this instance, no matter how much it hurts me, and believe me it does, I beg you to be brave and not to be beaten down by all these quite odd people demanding more film censorship.'

A doctor wrote to say, 'Morally no one is justified in imposing their particular views on another individual, and any person who attempts to do so is guilty of egocentrical arrogance. Each adult who has free will must also have self-determination and the right of personal censorship ... Medically it is well recognised that sexual offenders have had a lower exposure to sexual material than the average. Conversely those who have an usually restrictive attitude to sex, although not necessarily sex offenders, are very likely to suffer some degree of sexual psychopathology. So many patients suffer some degree of sexual block, that a more liberal attitude to such material is medically justified both at a psychological and a physiological level ...'

We also received support from organised groups for our proposals. The Defence of Literature and the Arts Society (of whose existence I had only recently learned) circulated a letter from its Chairman Will Hamling M.P. to all Councillors which was a welcome prop to those of my colleagues who intended to vote for our proposals. The British Federation of Film Societies, the Society for Education in Film and Television, the Independent Film Makers' Association, and the Greater London Arts Association all sent letters in support. On the eve of the vote, a group of Labour Members of Parliament led by Dr Colin Phipps expressed their agreement with the action we were proposing to take and with the need for government legislation.

As the date of the Council meeting drew near, discussion grew among Councillors and energetic lobbying went on. A letter from myself and the vice-chairman of the Film Viewing Board went to each Councillor asking them to support our proposals. Some Councillors had already got clear views on the way they would vote but others found themselves in difficulty. Two particular groups had problems. One were what I had named the 'nudge, nudge, wink, wink brigade', chiefly to be found among the Conservative men, whose characteristic approach to the subject of film censorship had been to sidle up to me and say, with many a confident nudge and wink, 'Of course, I can't see anything wrong with those films and I'm really on your side'. They were now called upon to put their views to the test in the vote and it was interesting to observe their growing evasiveness as the time approached. After all, it was one thing to be known as a bit of a lad who enjoyed a blue film and quite another to show publicly willingness for such films to be shown. Another group in difficulty on the Labour side were those consummate politicians who could not gauge which way the movement was going in their own party and among Labour supporters. A correct judgement would mean that they could be seen on the side of the progressive angels or, alternatively, as the upholders of clean socialist living. One or two of these were overcome by the problem and took refuge in absence from the Council Chamber on the night. Some Labour left wingers also had difficulty in deciding what was the correct left wing stance, but if 'pornography' had no ideological appeal, the emancipation of the cinema from 'establishment' control did and they generally voted for abolition. The majority of Councillors probably did not read the paper of evidence which we had so painstakingly assembled, but most knew instinctively where they stood on the issue. Within the Labour Group it had little to do with their other political views. Age had some influence, and so did religion: i.e. most older members and a strong Catholic contingent were opposed to the recommendations, but there were notable exceptions to both these generalisations. I was interested to see the emergence of an East London group of Labour Councillors opposing the recommendations; it seemed that puritanism dies hard for East Enders. On the other side were to be found the leading figures in the Education Authority and all the lecturers and teachers among us, lending credence to the need for open education and experience in their broadest sense. As votes were ticked off and members canvassed, it was clear that the result was going to be very close.

The day of the debate and vote in Council was one of high tension and excitement. *The Times*, the *Daily Telegraph* and the *Evening News* all devoted leaders to opposing our proposals, but the *Evening Standard* leaned in our favour. Mary Whitehouse, determined not to be upstaged, appeared in the Members' Lobby at County Hall as the guest of the Conservative Councillor Frank Smith, the self-appointed spokesman of the anti-pornography lobby, and members were invited to pay court to her. The Festival of Light staged a demonstration and prayer meeting on the steps of County Hall in pouring rain; testimony was given and hymns were sung to the stirring music of a Salvation Army Band. Pressure from newspaper reporters and local radio and television programmes was piling up with requests for interviews and statements. Fortunately, an efficient and friendly press officer was there to cope and to take some of the strain. For it was a strain. I knew we could not give in to all the pressures now and must put our case to the vote, but the hysteria and some of its grotesque manifestations made the going tough over those last hours.

The actual debate, broadcast live over the local radio, was something of an anticlimax for me. As Chairman of the Board which was only a sub-committee of a main Committee I had only the right to speak once in the debate and had to condense the whole case for the recommendations into ten minutes, aware that the Chairman of the Council, an opponent to my viewpoint, was not likely to allow me much leeway. I summarised the argument as best I could and ended with a quotation from John Milton's magnificent tract against censorship written in 1644: 'When God gave him [Adam] reason, He gave him freedom to choose, for reason is but choosing.'[1]That was for me the essence of the argument: the right to exercise our own judgement and to choose between the gold and the dross.

Speeches for and against the proposals went on for four hours. Most took the issue solely as a question of whether certain films of sex or violence ought to be banned. One councillor spoke of cinemas becoming 'cesspools of iniquity', another that London would become overnight the porn centre of the world, and a third that the Council must help parents to protect their teenage children from vile films and set a standard. Supporters of the proposal spoke of the incongruity of local councillors becoming guardians of the morals of their fellow citizens, the violent content of crime films for many years past, and the narrowness of the procensorship viewpoint. Two senior members agreed on the unsuitability of local councillors as censors but came to different decisions as to the way they would vote: one

[1]John Milton, 'Areopagitica: a speech for the liberty of unlicensed printing to the Parliament of England' in *Areopagitica and other Prose Works*, J.M. Dent & Sons Ltd, 1941, p. 18.

thought the GLC should give up its powers now, while the other said that a satisfactory substitute should be devised before that could be done. Two amendments were moved, one to tighten the regulations aimed at excluding the under eighteens from 'X' films, and the second asking for the situation to be reviewed in a year's time if censorship powers were given up. I decided to accept both. They were moderate and sensible and could help to secure more votes for the proposal.

Eventually at 2 a.m. the debate came to a close. The vote 'that the report be received' was called and the Council accepted the proposition by 50 votes to 42. Several people thought that the case had been won, but that was only a procedural device to accept the report so that the recommendations could be put. The crucial vote took place on the first recommendation. 'That the Council do cease to exercise its permissive power to censor films for persons over the age of 18 and that the rules of management be altered in accordance with this decision.' Members moved to the division lobbies to record their vote. To my surprise, I saw the Chairman, Dr David Pitt, and the Vice-Chairman and Deputy Chairman of the Council leave their positions on the dais and move towards the 'No' lobby. It was most unusual for the dais members to vote, although they were not debarred from so doing. Their judgement of the correct occasion on which to desert their traditionally impartial position seemed to me to be abysmal. It was clear that the vote was a tight one and that we were going to get very little Conservative support. Everything now depended on the strength of Labour 'no' votes and abstentions. The result was announced: 44 votes for the motion and 50 against, with three abstentions. We had lost. 41 Labour Councillors had voted for with only 2 Conservatives and one Liberal Councillor, 17 Labour and 33 Conservatives had voted against and 3 Labour Councillors had abstained. I was sad to see the Leader of the Council among the votes against as I knew of his strong belief in freedom of conscience. He afterwards told me that the existing law was too unsatisfactory in his view for us to take the step of giving up our powers, and I was told that he had been separately lobbied by the Home Office on this count. There was some consolation to be found in the number of women Councillors who voted for abolition by a proportion of two to one, demonstrating clearly that it was not women who felt the need to curb visual expressions of sexuality. 'Would you like your wife/daughter to see this film' was it seemed more an expression of the anxiety of men and not of their womenfolk. One of the two Conservative supporters was a distinguished woman, later to be deputy Chairman of the Council.

That was the end of the evening and of nearly two years' hard work. Immediately afterwards, I was asked by the media if I would resign my position as Chairman of the Film Viewing Board. I replied that there was now no point in my staying on in a job which I did not consider the Council should be doing, and that I wanted to devote my time to other more useful tasks. It only remained to pick up the bits and pieces. I wrote my letter of resignation the next day, answered reporters and interviewers on radio and television and, at greater leisure, the letters of condolence that came. Defeat had not been unexpected in view of the Labour Group's decision to allow a 'free' vote, but the effort was worthwhile. The debate had opened up the whole issue of film censorship to question and discussion. We had not been able to pull out the cornerstone of the system, but we had given the rickety structure a good shaking, and the impact in the longer run might be more effective than our defeat suggested.

Meanwhile, the sense of personal relief was considerable. I could now turn to the many difficult but absorbing problems of local government without the burden of abuse and sick fantasy directed against me which were the price of our attempt to give film censorship fundamental and rational consideration.

5

SEX AND OUTRAGE

Our strong and habitual interest in sex suggests that most people picking up this book will turn first to this Chapter. There is no doubt, in my experience, that sexual concerns are the driving force behind film censorship.

The sex act is a private affair concerning the most intimate of human relationships. To see it on the screen for the first time is strange and shocking. Feelings of embarassment and shame may follow the breaching of protective modesty. But even as the sight shocks and perhaps repels, it is also attractive and sexually arousing. At which point one of two reactions follows. Either the viewer begins to acknowledge and accept the emotions the film arouses and the feeling of being shocked lessens, or he or she feels that they should not be enjoying those feelings and begins to feel guilty. In the latter case, guilt calls forward strong efforts to control and suppress the 'wrong' feelings, and leads to a demand to ban the offending material. In other words, if a film is sexually arousing but the viewers feel it is against their moral code to find it so, they will judge it obscene and demand that it be censored. Such is the psychopathology of most film censorship.[1]

Acquaintance with sex in film habituates. As the first shock encounter subsides, what seemed so daring and outrageous becomes familiar. Then the boundary of acceptability shifts. Where yesterday the Hollywood couple could not be shown even fully clothed near a double bed and the heroine in any embrace had to keep one foot on the

[1]See D.L. Mosher, 'Sex differences, sex experience, sex guilt and explicitly sexual films' in *Journal of Social Issues*, 1973, Vol. 28. No. 3.

floor, today a naked couple may be shown embracing on the bed. To many accustomed to the old standards, the shifting line is a matter for reproach. Those who now accept the extra inches of flesh intertwined may feel emancipated, but if their adherence to a prohibitive code of sexual morality is strong the feelings of guilt are greater and they feel that they and others have been 'corrupted'. And since so many films made for the sexual content build on sex fantasies, particularly those of men, they play directly on the deepest and most suppressed images we have. Sado-masochism, for example, (sometimes called the English vice) is a very common theme and fantasy for both men and women; its appeal may explain the strong and obsessive interest that *The Times* newspaper[1] has recently devoted to it as a basis for film censorship.

Many prohibitions are reserved for, or justified by, the so-called abnormal, or perverse sex acts. For some, 'perversion' includes homosexuality, for others oral sex or sodomy. Further down the road come incest, paedophilia and bestiality. It would be hard to find anyone for whom there was not at least one manifestation of sex felt to be outrageous if shown on the screen. The threshold of tolerance and acceptability is different for each person and moves from time to time for all of us. That is why the pursuit of the boundaries of acceptability is so fascinating for both film-makers and the public. Who draws the line, and where, is a subject of never-failing interest.

Sexual mores are closely bound up with social ones. Pre-marital sex, for example, has been accorded a radical change in film treatment over the last 20 years. So has homosexuality. The British Board of Film Censors' rule that in intercourse the women must never be shown on top of the man[2] speaks volumes for the censors' view of the

[1] 'The Pornography of Hatred', Leader in *The Times*, 30/1/76.
[2] See Chapter 7, p. 115. However, this rule now appears to have disappeared, judging by the scene in 'Network' which was awarded an 'AA' certificate in 1976.

75

respective roles of the two sexes. The defenders of censorship are equally concerned with social as with sexual life styles. When films show, for example, casual sexual relationships, homosexuality, or black and white love affairs without comment or condemnation, they reflect a change in life style and values which may be unacceptable and threatening to the upholders of an earlier status quo. And since social values are equally bound up with political ones, it is not fanciful to assert that a demand to censor, say, a sex scene between a black man and a white woman is as much an illustration of the person's political view of the position of black people in society as it is of his or her threshold of sexual shockability.

Shock and outraged modesty which lead to cries of 'filth' and 'smut' are one firm basis for the demand for film censorship. The conviction that the showing of films with a high sexual content is morally wrong is another. The argument here centres round the view that the sex act is legitimate only when carried out for the purpose of procreation and as an act of conjugal love when it then serves a higher moral and spiritual purpose. It is also based on the many Bible injunctions against 'lewdness' and fornication of which St Paul's epistle to the Ephesians (Chapter 5) is as good an example as any, 'Be ye therefore followers of God, as dear children and walk in love, as Christ also hath loved us ... But fornication, and all uncleanliness, or covetousness, let it not be once named among you ... neither filthiness, nor foolish talking, nor jesting, what are not convenient, but rather giving of thanks. For this ye know, that no whoremonger, nor unclean person, nor covetous man, who is an idolater, hath any inheritance in the kingdom of Christ and of God ... And have no fellowship with the unfruitful works of darkness, but rather reprove them. For it is a shame even to speak of those things which are done of them in secret.'

Once the Biblical injunctions are accepted, no further argument is necessary. As Commissioner Keating put it in his dissenting report to the U.S. Commission on Obscenity and Pornography, 'For those who believe in God, in His absolute supremacy as the Creator and Lawgiver of life, in the dignity and destiny which He has conferred upon the human person, in the moral code that governs sexual activity – for those who believe in these 'things', no argument against pronography should be necessary.'[1]

The conviction that 'pornography' is ethically or morally wrong is not however confined to religious persons. David Holbrook is an avowed humanist who argues that 'pornography' degrades and debases sex, 'Nothing is more reductive of human dignity than mere sexuality, for being thus reductive, it destroys that capacity for 'spiritual intentionality' that we seek in love.'[2] Further, 'There is a sexual revolution, which one can trace back to Chaucer ... which is rooted in human feeling for the value of human beings. And there is a pseudo-sexual revolution, whose basis is in a hatred of being human. The humiliation of the body, the objectification of the voyeur, and the sadism of visual rape serve the latter. So, I believe, the solution to the breakdown of our culture into cultural perversion, with all its destructive effects, is to develop legislation by which we can prohibit any acts of public exhibitionism in which the genitals are revealed, and in which sexual acts involving the genitals take place.'[3] (However, he does hastily add, 'It should also be possible to make a proviso that, in certain works of art, where the overall creative intention of the artist demands, it should be possible to accept total nudity ...')

Holbrook's view that sexuality is only permissible when it serves love and creativity is closely akin to the religious view earlier outlined which sees justifiable sex only where there is a moral and spiritual purpose. Sex for fun is out. Sex fantasies are seen as wholly destructive and to be

[1] Statement by Charles H. Keating, Jr. in *Report of the Commission on Obscenity and Pornography*, op. cit., p. 515.
[2] D. Holbrook, *The Pseudo-Revolution*, Tom Stacey Ltd., 1972, p. 54.
[3] D. Holbrook, op. cit., p. 192.

77

suppressed, lest they injure emotional maturation and promote contempt and sadism for the sex object. Holbrook's attack is vehement and humourless. He puts sex on a pedestal and idolizes it but only within the context of a noble and spiritual love. Nothing less will satisfy him and where it appears as trivial or serving only physical pleasure, it must be firmly suppressed. Holbrook's approach rests partly on the often quoted view of D.H. Lawrence that 'pornography is the attempt to insult sex, to do dirt on it'. But Lawrence did not want to suppress all sexual material. He inveighed most strongly against the censorship that covered the 'dirty little secret of sex' and 'the grey ones [who] will pass and will commend floods of evasive pornography and will suppress every outspoken word'.[1] Lawrence was for openness in sex and condemned the underworld of secrecy about it. Holbrook's condemnation of all open portrayals of sex seems to come closer to the puritan view that pleasure is decadent.

The puritan view also accords with the 'Nero fiddled while Rome burns' argument. Here, the decline of a society is linked to over-indulgence and a decadent pursuit of pleasure for its own sake; only where the mores are stern and heroic and self-indulgent pleasure is denied can a society advance to greatness. The usual example given is that the excesses of Weimar Germany led to the emergence of Nazi Germany. However, this example is odd, to say the least, because Nazi Germany is a perfect example of a society extolling effort and heroic purpose and practising a stringent system of censorship which was totally wicked and morally bankrupt. However, the notion persists and is frequently advanced, as for example by *The Times* columnist Ronald Butt, 'Not for the first time in the rise and decline of civilisation, or phases of civilisation, has the debauching of currency gone hand in hand with the debauching of personal standards and people are encouraged to retreat into acceptance of actual behaviour and

[1] D.H. Lawrence, *Sex Literature and Censorship*, Heinemann, 1955.

'recreation' which, in normal times would have been regarded as intolerably depraved.'[1]

Lord Devlin has advocated the censorship of material which would threaten the shared morality of society.[2] In his view, a healthy morality is essential to the well-being of society and should not be harmed by corrupting material. Sometimes too, 'pornography' is seen as an almost conscious left wing plot to undermine and overthrow society or indeed the State. A GLC Councillor, for example, wrote to the *Daily Telegraph* expressing the view in relation to films that 'One only needs to look back into history to see how nations became decadent in the first instance by the decline in moral values and I cannot help but wonder if the 'moderates' are in fact trying to undermine our society for their own ends',[3] and a local paper headlined a feature on film censorship 'A leftish plot to destroy our society'.[4] Mary Whitehouse has also 'accused the "far left" of promoting pornography to destroy Britain's morale and character'.[5]

Castigation of 'pornography' is not, however, confined to the natural conservatives and upholders of the status quo. There is a feeling among many socialists that permissiveness in sexual affairs and its manifestations on the screen do not fit well into an ideal socialist order. In part, such sentiments derive from the drive of early working class socialists to improve and educate themselves, an effort requiring self discipline and abstinence from drink and indulgence. Francis Place, for example, one of the reformers working for the repeal of Acts prohibiting trades unions in the 1820s, avowed that 'I cannot, like many other men, go to a tavern. I hate taverns and tavern company.'[6]

[1] 'The Vicious Circles of Pornography' in *The Times*, 13/12/73.
[2] J. Devlin, 'The Enforcement of Morals' in *Maccabean and other lectures*, 1965.
[3] J. Tatham in *Daily Telegraph*, 30/11/73.
[4] *Orpington Times*, 6/12/73.
[5] 'Whitehouse attack on leftist porn' in *Sunday Times*, 19/10/75.
[6] E.P. Thompson, *The Making of the English Working Class*, Penguin Books, 1968, p. 63.

Many of the early trades unions had rules prohibiting and fining drinking and swearing, and urging a strict code of sober conduct and behaviour.[1] The non-conformist churches, which provided a chapel background for so many British socialists, bristled with moral injunctions against profanity, drink, and sex. Like the seventeenth century puritans who closed down the playhouses in Cromwell's time and curbed many of the ancient country fairs and festivals, the Weslyan methodists a century later had prohibited card playing, theatre going, and 'profane' songs and dancing.'[2]

At the end of the Victorian era, the Fabians too thought the leisure pursuits of the people were undesirable. Sydney Olivier in his first Fabian essay on the moral basis of socialism saw the workers as 'generally coarse in their habits; they lack intelligence in their amusements and refinement in their tastes. The worst of this is the popularity of boozing and gambling and allied forms of excitement, with their outcomes in violence and meanness. But once society has ensured for man the opportunity for satisfying his primary needs – once it has ensured him a healthy body and a wholesome life, his advance in the refinements of social morality, in the conception and satisfaction of his secondary and more distinctly human desires, is solely and entirely a matter of education.'[3] Oliviers' faith in socialism and education as the answer to the aesthetic and moral poverty of nineteenth century working class life was echoed in the fastidiousness of many middle class Fabian intellectuals. Beatrice Webb expressed the view that both the upper and lower classes were 'oversexed' and only the 'respectable working class, middle class and professional life'[4] showed a correct concentration on more sober pursuits.

[1] E.P. Thompson, op. ci., pp. 457-9
[2] Ibid., p. 449.
[3] S. Olivier, 'Moral' in *Fabian Essays in Socialism 1889* 1948 edn., Allen & Unwin, p. 116.
[4] Beatrice Webb, *Our Partnership*, Longmans Green & Co., 1948, p. 448.

She disapproved of her fellow Fabian H.G. Wells' advocacy of 'free love' and opposed 'sexual emotion for its own sake and not for the sake of rearing children'.[1] Wells strongly favoured a more open and free expression of sexuality. Bernard Shaw took as his ideal of the highest human development the wholly cerebral elders in *Back to Methuselah*, although in *Pygmalion* he clearly had more than a sneaking sympathy for his unregenerate dustman, Alfred Doolittle, the self-styled champion of the undeserving poor. Shaw favoured realism, honest sensuality, even bawdiness in the arts, but opposed romanticism and the 'systematic idolatry of sensuousness'. 'The pleasures of the senses I can sympathise with and share; but the substitution of sensuous ecstacy for intellectual activity and honesty is the very devil.'[2]

Echoes of Olivier, Beatrice Webb, H.G. Wells, and Shaw's attitudes are very much with us today among left wingers of all varieties. As cash benefits, social services, and universal education seem to bring insufficient uplifting of the people's tastes, there is an uneasiness about manifestations in entertainment and films of coarseness and licentiousness whose popularity had previously been attributed to the lack of education and low material standards of the masses. Thus, while the conservatives see in 'pornography' an undermining of the traditional values of society, some of the left find it a disappointing relic of less enlightened capitalist days which has not yet disappeared.

To complete this account of the attitudes of various social groups towards sex in films and censorship, it is important to consider the views of women and, in particular, of women's groups. There is a very marked ambivalence in attitudes. The traditional view of women from Biblical days onwards has been of creatures inferior and subservient to men. In the best conditions, they enjoyed a status within the family of protection by men as objects of

[1] Ibid., p. 360.
[2] G.B. Shaw, Preface to *Three Plays for Puritans*, Penguin Books, 1946, pp. xxxi-ii.

domestic esteem and romantic idealisation. In the worst conditions, they were brutalized and exploited by men, driven to hard work at low wages or to prostitution and denied an independent economic position. The feminists fought for a greater independence for women, both economically and socially, and for their freedom from exploitation by men, either in a domestic situation or, more crudely, as sexual objects. The struggle has taken various forms and includes the protection of women from prostitution, women's control of their own property after marriage, the drive for birth control, for easier divorce laws, and, most recently, for abortion law reform. In all these efforts, men are frequently seen as brutal and rapacious exploiters of women, seeking to enforce their sexual as well as their economic domination over women. The context is readily extended to sex films which are seen by many women as an exploitation of their sex by men for their own gratification. This reading is as readily acceptable to women content with the traditional domestic role as to the most ardent activists in the women's movement striving to liberate their own sex. As sex films are so often the uninhibited sex fantasies of men, they can readily be seen as exploitative of women. Equally, however, they can be read as a trap for men, forcing them into a rigid and conventionally masculine sexual stereotype in which the values of domination and brutality are pressed while denying men's warmth and tenderness. If 'liberation' is the cry, it is clearly necessary for both sexes to break out from the crude stereotypes in which our society still persists in shaping their sexual and social destiny. The suppression of one kind of manifestation of crude sexuality in films will hardly help the emancipation of both men and women, but will reaffirm the view that men are coarse beasts whose brutish instincts must be repressed. The answer may lie in the work of more women as film directors. Joan Micklin Silver's film *Hester Street* for example gave a very different view of the bragging but weaker husband and the quiet strength of the wife than the usual male oriented view of man/woman relationships.

I have dwelt at some length on attitudes towards sexuality and its exhibition on the film screen because I believe the objection to it comes from the complex of psychological, moral and socio-political attitudes which the viewer brings to his or her viewing rather than the intrinsic merit or otherwise of the material seen. In other words, 'pornography' is very much in the eye of the beholder, and as almost everyone has a line or limit on what they regard as acceptable sexual manifestation, it is as easy to be against 'pornography' as to be against 'sin', although as hard in one case as in the other to define exactly what is meant.

However the public arguments are very often conducted differently. It is alleged that 'pornography' is directly harmful and that viewing it will lead to criminal actions such as rape and sex crimes as well as more conventional criminal behaviour. If pornographic films cause social harm an objective case for banning them exists, and it is therefore necessary to examine the arguments in some detail. It should also be noted that the phrase 'deprave and corrupt' which defiines obscenity in both the Obscene Publications Act and the Theatres Act is generally interpreted by the same criteria.

An examination of the theme of social harm may call on evidence from clinical case studies, from psychological treatises on sex and on delinquency, and from statistical surveys of the correlation between sexually explicit materials and crime. Clinical evidence comes from doctors and psychiatrists who have treated patients with psycho-sexual disorders and emotional disturbance. Dr G.B. Barker, a consultant psychiatrist, contributed to the Arts Council Working Party report on the obscenity laws the view that 'In my experience I have never met any patient whose condition was caused by 'exposure to sexuality', but I have met innumerable examples of ignorance, fear and ideas of guilt causing much neurotic illness and unhappiness.'[1]

[1] *The Obscenity Laws*, Report by the Working Party set up by a Conference convened by the Chairman of the Arts Council of Great Britain, André Deutsch, 1969.

Dr Brian Richards, a general practitioner with a particular interest in sexual problems, offered evidence in support of the therapeutic value of *Inside Linda Lovelace* at the Old Bailey, on the grounds that (sexual) 'deviation can be relieved by such processes as masturbation during which fantasy situations are enacted in the person's mind'.[1] On the other side of the argument, in this particular case, Dr Mary Macaulay, Consultant to a Marriage Guidance Council, pointed to 'many tragic histories of young wives whose marriages are broken because their husbands are impotent, only receiving sexual stimulation and pleasure from masturbation',[2] (presumably stimulated by 'pornographic' materials). Dr Macaulay evidently considered that pornography leading to masturbation perpetuated sexual disorders, while Dr Richards expressed the view that it could be a relief and preferable to the alternatives of severe repression or the actual acting out of fantasies. But whichever side of the argument they fall, while these opinions on clinical experience are of value, they are limited by their basis in the abnormal pathology of sexual or other emotional disorders.

More important is the increased understanding we derive from investigations into normal sexual behaviour. Thanks to Kinsey[3] in the 1940s and 1950s and to Masters and Johnson[4] in the 1960s, we have a much more accurate understanding today of normal sexual behaviour than in the past. It was on their kind of work that the extensive studies commissioned by the American Commission on Obscenity and Pornography built. The Effects Panel of the Commission instigated a programme of research on the kinds of effect arising from exposure to sexually explicit

[1] Letter to *The Times*, 5/2/76.
[2] Letter to *The Times*, 3/2/76.
[3] A.C. Kinsey, W.B. Pomeroy, and C.E. Martin, *Sexual Behaviour in the Human Male*, 1948, A.C. Kinsey, W.B. Pomeroy, C.E. Martin, and P.H. Gebhard, *Sexual Behaviour in the Human Female*, 1956.
[4] W.H. Masters, and V.E. Johnson, *Human Sexual Response*, 1966.

materials which included a major national study based on interviews with more than 3,000 people chosen on the basis of a random sample throughout the U.S.A. The results of these researches may be summarised as follows.[1] First, as to the effect on sexual behaviour, it was found that 'erotic stimuli' caused sexual arousal in large numbers of both men and women, more strongly amongst the younger, better educated, and sexually experienced. Continual exposure to these materials over two weeks not surprisingly resulted in satiation and diminution of interest which could only briefly be restimulated by novel material, but the researchers reported a partial recovery of interest after a break of two months. As to the effects on sexual behaviour, no change was reported in the majority of people. A minority reported either temporarily increased sexual activity, mostly by the sexually experienced with their usual partners, or (a smaller proportion) a decrease in sexual activity. Little or no effect was found to have taken place in the attitudes of those studied towards sexuality or sexual morality. As to the emotional reaction towards the material shown, it was found that the responses varied greatly according to the psychological make-up of the people concerned. The multiple response of attraction and repulsion was common, especially in those unfamiliar with sexual material. The verdict 'obscene' was most likely to be given by persons who were older, less educated, religiously active, less experienced with erotic materials, and suffering from feelings of sexual guilt.

Comparing normal with delinquent youth, the Panel found that general and widespread experience of sexual materials was similar for both delinquent and non-delinquent young people, but that sex offenders had had less adolescent (though not adult) experience with erotic materials than other adults. The Panel pointed out that massive increases in sex crimes had not occurred since

[1] *Report of the Commission on Obscenity and Pornography*, op. cit., pp. 26-7.

erotic materials had become more available. Arrests for crimes of rape in the U.S. had increased among adults but had decreased for juveniles. The Panel and the Commission concluded with the careful but massive opinion that 'In sum, empirical evidence designed to clarify the question has found no reliable evidence to date that exposure to explicit sexual materials plays a significant role in the causation of delinquent or criminal behaviour among youth or adults. The Commission cannot conclude that exposure to erotic materials is a factor in the causation of sex crime or sex delinquency.'[1]

The experience in Denmark is of direct relevance to this measurement of 'effects', because restrictions on the availability of written sexual materials were removed in 1967 and on pictorial material, including films, in 1969 (both excepting the case of children). Berl Kutchinsky, Director of the Institute of Criminal Science in Copenhagen, has made some interim analysis of the effects of this change on sex crimes in an article published in 1973[2] and his larger study of the subject is currently awaited. Kutchinsky observed that the number of sex offences in Denmark had begun to fall before restrictions were removed on sexual materials and that the fall had continued in the years following. Between 1959 and 1970, offences of 'peeping' had decreased by 80%, verbal indecency by 71%, physical indecency towards girls and child molestation by 59%, exhibitionism by 58% and offences against women by 56%. Only crimes of rape had shown no decrease. Kutchinsky thought that the fall in offences towards women or exhibitionism might have been attributable to the general social climate in Denmark. Child molesters and 'peepers' were in a different category and pornography might well have had a beneficial substitution effect on the former who

[1] Ibid., p. 139.
[2] B. Kutchinsky, 'The effect of easy availability of pornography on the incidence of sex crimes: the Danish experience' in *Journal of Social Issues*, 1973, vol. 29, no. 3.

were usually sexually deprived individuals unable to secure for themselves ordinary sexual satisfaction. Nor has the Danish population become obsessed with pornography. Kutchinsky has pointed out that in Copenhagen today 'porno shops are almost exclusively situated in tourist districts; and apart from one weekly magazine with a circulation of 10,000 copies (for comparison, Donald Duck circulates 212,000) the sparing text in Danish porno magazines is in English, French and German, not Danish ... as much as 95% of all the pornography produced in Denmark goes abroad.'[1]

It is also worth pointing to the research survey carried out by Maurice Yaffe, a psychologist at the Maudsley Hospital specialising on this subject, on behalf of Lord Longford's privately appointed Commission.[2] Yaffe made a wide ranging analysis of numerous research studies on the impact of pornography on sex offenders and· concluded that scientific research had not yet produced sufficient evidence one way or the other on which to base firm conclusions. His personal judgement, however, expressed in a number of court cases where he appeared for the defence, was that sexual films and books did not lead to deviant acts but could be of positive and educative value.

The conclusions of the American Commission and of Kutchinsky do not go unchallenged. The American Commission itself was signed by 15 of its 18 members, among them professors and practitioners of law, sociology, and psychiatry. Three members, – a Jesuit priest, a Methodist minister and President Nixon's nominee Charles Keating – dissented radically from its conclusion that restrictions on materials for adults should be removed, and a fourth, a rabbi, thought that a study over a 5 year period to assess long term effects should be made before restrictions were removed. The three dissentients commissioned another psychologist, Victor Cline, to review the research carried out by the effects panel. Cline found the research had

[1] Letter to *The Guardian*, 16/6/76.
[2] *Pornography: the Longford Report*, Coronet Books, 1972.

serious flaws, omissions, and grave shortcomings, and a major bias in the reporting. His review has provided ammunition for the anti-pornography crusaders, so that the battle over 'evidence' can be continued.

Protagonists of the view that there is a causal link between sexual materials and sex crimes are few on the ground among the professionals. The main one appears to be Dr J.H. Court, lecturer in psychology at Flinders University, South Australia, and a member of the Australian Festival of Light, who flew all the way to England at the request and expense of the National Viewers' and Listeners' Association to give evidence at a recent obscenity trial and whose views are frequently cited by Mary Whitehouse as the best of the experts on the subject. Dr Court, in an article awarded prominence in *The Times*.[1] describes the effects in Denmark of easily available pornography as 'inconclusive' because the final change did not take place until 1969, but then dismisses what evidence there is on the grounds that 'in view of the controversy that has surrounded Denmark's policies, it would be safer to look elsewhere ...' He points to an increase in the reporting of serious sex crimes such as rape in Britain, the U.S.A., and Australia in recent years and alleges that it cannot be ascribed only to an increase in reporting offences by victims. He concludes that 'while we may allow that a naively simplistic cause and effect explanation cannot be offered ... we cannot ignore the complex social pathology which has been facilitated by the growth of the pornographic industry'. Court correctly points out that sex research is in its infancy, but leans heavily on prejudice to counteract such evidence that we have when he asserts 'it is premature to invoke evidence which runs counter to the intuitive good sense of centuries'. He concedes that 'some of the more sexually explicit manuals and books can have an educative or therapeutic function in some cases' but

[1]'Time to speak out against the idea that pornography can be a good thing' in *The Times*, 3/8/76.

distinguishes sex instruction material, which is useful when 'well chosen', from 'erotica' designed for titillation among normal males which appears to be acceptable if not desirable, and from true pornography which is distinguished for him by 'the inherent messages of hate and degradation of women', in which all standards in sexual relations are violated. Such works amount to disease and pollution in our society and should therefore be eliminated by 'effective quality control of literature and films' (a term Court, like the Festival of Light, prefers to censorship). Court's thesis really links up three separate strands which go to form the basis for censoring sexual materials. The first is any scraps or inferences of association with crime that he can find and gaps in the conclusive evidence on the other side. The second is the Holbrook view on the pornography of hate, which degrades women as sex objects. The third is a fall back on 'commonsense' which might almost be described in this context as a last ditch of prejudice, ignorance, and bigotry over the ages since Biblical times.

In many ways, the Longford *Report* view is more straightforward and honest. It recommends that the criterion for judging obscenity in films should be what outrages contemporary standards of decency or humanity accepted by the public at large.[1] With this definition, we are back with what people feel to be outrageous. One might add, as Lord Melbourne said in another context, there is no damned merit in it. And that brings us back to the basic reason why people wish to ban films, because they are shocked by them. But Longford's criteria runs into the very real problem that contemporary standards vary so greatly that there is no reliable way of interpreting public opinion on the subject. What is outrageous to one person will be readily acceptable to another. The search for 'standards' in our present fluid society is extraordinarily difficult as between the young and the old, men and women, the

[1] *Pornography: the Longford Report*, Coronet Books, 1972, p. 427.

better and the less well educated, to name but a few ways of categorizing people.

The Longford thesis does however bring us face to face with the main question: why, if some find a film shocking, should they demand that others not be allowed to see it? If the best evaluation shows that there is scant evidence of the dire effects of viewing sex films on sexual and delinquent behaviour, why should some be denied the opportunity to see what others may not wish to see?

6

THE FEAR OF VIOLENCE

Discussions on film censorship generally start with sex but, sooner or later, someone is sure to say 'It's not the sex I mind, it's the violence.' The comment has several meanings. The most immediate is that violent actions seen on the screen may be both shocking and distressing. Underlying is the view that violence is unwholesome, undesirable, and harmful to both individual and social relations. For the conscientious liberal in particular, for whom sexual activity is a healthy and happy ideal which can be enjoyed or at least tolerated on the screen, violence poses a threat. The liberal life-style of personal emancipation, loving and caring relationships, and the enjoyment of an ordered but free society cannot co-exist with disorder, brutality and their accompanying squalor. Violence portrayed on the screen is a reminder of the dark forces which can all too easily overwhelm fragile personal and social structures. To say that one is against violence on the screen is to reaffirm opposition to violent action and to the suffering caused by it. From there it is easy to take the next step, which is to say that because violence should not exist, it should not be seen on film screens either, and, by another jump in reasoning, it should therefore be banned or censored off our screens. By advocating that violence should be censored from films, the would-be censor is at one stroke removing the source of his distress and justifying his action as thoroughly social and beneficial. Personal comfort and the advancement of social objectives can thus be happily combined.

Honesty must, however, prompt further questioning. Much of the widespread violence in films is highly popular and thoroughly enjoyable. If it were not, war films, crime films, and westerns would not be the staple fare of screen entertainment. Certain themes of violence reappear again and again. The hunter and the hunted is one, with the hero as the hunted, law abiding man who turns on his pursuers. Who can deny the appeal of Gary Cooper facing out his pursuers in *High Noon*, Marlon Brando slugging it out with the corrupt union leader in *On the Waterfront*, or that classic situation where the mild mannered hero turns on the bully to win his manhood spurs ('I'm coming in to get you')? No less popular are films where the hero is the hunter usually bringing bad men to justice. There are endless police dramas which start with a crime and its detection and end in a car chase through the streets followed by a shoot-out with armed police. The tough, revolver-toting Sweeney are a long way from the original unarmed P.C. Dixon who was killed in *The Blue Lamp*. Outlaws practising violence are also much admired, whether historical (*Robin Hood*) or latter day and glamorous (*Butch Cassidy*). The violence of natural forces and the fight to overcome them is another popular theme, ranging from Hemingwayesque encounters between man and beast, to *Moby Dick*, *The Birds* and *King Kong*. Subduing supernatural forces by violent means provides the basis for science fiction films and for horror sagas all the way from Frankenstein and Dracula, through the Hammer Films of the 1950s to *The Exorcist* and a rediscovered interest in the violence of the devil, all of which induce highly enjoyable shivers of fear in the cinema audience.

In spite of the frequent diatribes against sexual violence, it is clear that a degree of sexual violence in films is also popular. Heroes are shown smacking their girl friends in the face (Cagney), spanking them (Wayne), and overcoming their resistance by superior strength in sexual encounters. The pleasures of male conquest and female submission in sex are often portrayed on screen to the delight of both sexes. The fantasy of rape may also be attractive (witness *King Kong*), equally to women as to men, provided the action is far removed from the pain and humiliation of its reality.

Humourous violence is also prominent. Slapstick comedy, the impossible feats of James Bond, Donald Duck, and Tom and Jerry all play their part in entertainment.

If all this violence is a daily part of films which we enjoy, how does the call to ban violence from films come about? When does violence go sour on us and become uncomfortable? Clearly some films do overstep the mark of audience tolerance in terms of the violence they portray. *Straw Dogs* is an excellent example. It contains many of the popular ingredients for a film of its kind. The hero is a sensitive intellectual who is innocent of the dark and primitive forces of violence manifested by the rural villagers. They challenge him by bullying, the sexual takeover of his wife who is an ambiguous character emanating from and partly allied to the rustics, and a final attack on his home. He is eventually obliged to face his attackers, defend wife and hearth, and overcome an all out assault by viciously violent means. He emerges a hero who has proved his manhood and gained respect through violent combat. It is the theme of numerous successful westerns, particularly popular in American movies. If Peckinpah's film was so comparable to many others, it is important to try and understand why there was so much outcry about it. Possibly the 'rape' scene was too explicit, or the wife's acceptance of it was too ambiguous, or perhaps the actual details of the attack were both too horrific (the primitive metal mantrap) and too domestic (fire and boiling water). Again the setting of the film in what should have been the familiar and comforting English countryside with its portrayal of hostile and aggressive inhabitants may be too unsettling to take. What is clear, however, is that theme, plot, and characterisation were typical of many popular and acclaimed films and it is only in detail, mood, or context that we may find the clue to the furore that it caused. In this film the pleasurable aspects of violent encounter appear to have been outweighed by unpleasant ones and the thin line between tolerable and intolerable fear, acceptable and unacceptable fantasy, breached to produce a reaction of outrage and disgust. And, as we have seen with sex films, a reaction of outrage leads to a call for banning and censorship.

The proposition that violence should be censored from films is also interesting in a historical context, because violence has been the staple diet of all art forms over the centuries. Greek and Jacobean drama, the Nordic sagas, *Beowulf*, Picasso's *Guernica*, and innumerable depictions of that supremely violent act the Crucifixion in paintings only begin to illustrate the point. Are there particular reasons why violence should not be seen in films?

One possible explanation is the easy capacity of film making techniques to simulate horrific effects and to highlight them. We may be frightened by 'monsters' from Frankenstein and Dracula to the Daleks and their less lovable science fiction colleagues fashioned with all the expertise of the make-up and props departments. Scenes of warfare, rape, torture and murder can be shown in close-up detail and with greater physical verisimilitude than on the stage. Clever use of cameras and film cutting techniques also serve to heighten tension and fear. All this technical expertise increases the shock and horror of the presentation of violence.

Another factor is the artistry of the film maker who can transform acts of violence which in truth are sudden, short, and squalid into fantasies of considerable and elaborate beauty, rather as the bullfighter's art transforms a brutal act of animal slaughter into an elegant ritual. The reality of violence is hidden as the art of the cameraman spins out webs of fantasy which are both fascinating and deeply disturbing.

Certainly, the capacity to portray the effects of injury and death in detail on the screen can be very frightening. Parents seek to protect their children from frightening experiences, and certain films are for the same reason classified as unsuitable for children. Is it possible to apply the same reasoning to films shown to adult audiences, to come to an objective view as to what is too nasty or upsetting to show? An affirmative seems to be an easy answer until we examine the matter further. If we draw up a list of taboo subjects and treatments, the classification quickly breaks down. Frankenstein-style monsters for example do not frighten those to whom they appear unreal. Death in any particular form does not in itself qualify. Nor does the number of deaths. It greatly depends on the context, who is receiving the violence, who is handing it out, and how the dramatic impact is built up. The treatment of killing in *Bonnie and Clyde* or *The Godfather*, for example, is not distressing although it is explicit. *A Clockwork Orange*, on the other hand, is less explicit in showing death but more upsetting. The answer to this paradox to the accepted wisdom on the subject lies with the reactions of the audience and not necessarily with the amount of explicit detail. *A Clockwork Orange, Straw Dogs, Soldier Blue* are shocking and distressing because they reach into and disturb our emotional lives: they invade our privacy. John Fraser describes this category of film as 'the violation movie',[1] a violation which takes place because of 'the real or threatened gross invasion of the privacy of "decent" people by violent men, an invasion in which rape as well as murder may be a real possibility'. We do not identify with the victims of *Bonnie and Clyde*, or *Butch Cassidy*, but rather with the violators themselves who appear as romantic outcasts and outlaws. But we do identify with the victims of the Clockwork Orange gang, whether the old tramp or the couple whose house is clearly signposted as 'Home'. Further reflection will show how often individuals react differently to films. To quote two personal experiences, a colleague once told me of a scene in a film which he said had upset him more than anything else he had ever seen. I had seen the film but could not even remember the sequence to which he referred. He had

[1] John Fraser, *Violence in the Arts*, Cambridge University Press, 1974, p. 17.

evidently identified himself in the situation he had seen in a way which I had not. I once fainted from the tension and horror of *All Quiet on the Western Front* in the middle of a surprised cinema audience which was not similarly affected. Such contrary experiences are manifold.

Clearly, the amount of violent detail shown does not on its own prescribe a certain level of fear from which we need protection. The capacity of each individual to empathise with the victims of the violence seen is a necessary factor to turn an unpleasant experience into an outrageous one. For that to happen, Fraser has suggested that the victims must be familiar and preferably innocent figures with whom the viewer may identify either in terms of physical appearance or working role.[1] There is a parallel experience in reality: violence practised against a secure and recognisable family background in our own society will shock more deeply than when the victims are depersonalised in portrayal, for example, Asians ('yellow-bellies', 'gooks') or young vagrants ('layabouts') or simply 'aliens' against whom we are fighting a 'just' war ('huns', 'wops', etc.).

There may also be a stage when identification with the victims is so strong as to condition social attitudes. The most recent research on the effects of television viewing in America has indicated that the constant repetition in crime series of acts of violence has caused television viewers to empathise with the victims to such an extent that they have a heightened sense of fear and mistrust of other people.[2] The viewers were found to overestimate violence in society and to accept passively the need for greater force used by the police in the process of law enforcement in order to protect them. This study places emphasis on the effects of fear generated by violent films and suggests that viewers need protection from violent crime films

[1] John Fraser, op. cit., pp. 58-60.
[2] Research by Prof. G. Gerbner and Dr. L. Gross of the Annenberg School of Communications, University of Pennsylvania summarised in Stacy Marking, 'The Case of the Frightened Viewer' *The Guardian*, 12/8/76.

which in America occupy 20% of prime viewing time on television.

Thus far we have dealt with the capacity of films with a violent content to arouse distress and fear from which we need protection. A much more usual reason advanced for censoring violence on screen is concerned with the glorification of violent acts which are thought to encourage a society in which such acts are condoned and approved. Violence can be both acceptable and exciting when we consider the approval given to championing boxers and wrestlers, fox-hunting or, for that matter, anti-foxhunting campaigns. At some point, however, there is anxiety that the approval of violence becomes anti-social. There may be a stage at which it is feared the romantic heroes and outlaws of the screen provide too close a model for actual action. In particular, if violence is seen as an exciting and justifiable way of solving the problems of society through revolution (whether from the left or the right), then it indeed becomes a threat to the forces of order and stability. We are very prone to make heroes out of warriors, but too great a romantic attachment may lead to tolerance of armed action in our society. Similarly, the choice of violent action to solve individual problems so often featured in movies may present too close a model for its imitation and approval in domestic and personal life.

Beyond this generalised fear of violence as an easy option to problem solving lies a more specific and longstanding concern about the actual effect that viewing violence may have in stimulating individuals to aggressive acts. The fear that criminal activity will be increased if potential criminals or even ordinary citizens are stimulated by films to emulate what they have seen is a popular one. It is in this area that strenuous attempts by social scientists have been made to establish the truth of such fears, and there is an abundant literature on the subject which concentrates particularly on children and young people. In 1958, for example, a major study on the effects of television on children examined the effect of television's crime and

97

detective series on children and concluded that 'Television is unlikely to cause aggressive behaviour although it could precipitate it in those few children who are emotionally disturbed. On the other hand, there was little support for the view that programmes of violence are beneficial; we found that they aroused aggression as often as they discharged it.'[1] And again, 'Seeing violence on television is not likely to turn well-adjusted children into aggressive delinquents; there must be a predisposition for them to be affected in this way.'[2] Numerous studies before and since have reiterated these conclusions. A UNESCO survey in 1961 found that ' ... on the evidence so far available, it is extremely difficult – indeed virtually inpossible – to establish that cinema has a direct influence on juvenile delinquency.'[3] A British survey on the relation of television to delinquency examined the research carried out some years later and concluded that 'The whole weight of research and theory in the juvenile delinquency field would suggest that the mass media, except just possibly in the case of a very small number of pathological individuals, are never the sole cause of delinquent behaviour. At most they may play a contributory role, and that a minor one.'[4]

The possibility that children may be stimulated to aggressive acts by seeing violent films is, however, acknowledged by the behavioural scientists. Studies made for a recent American report on the impact of televised violence found that children could be instigated to individual acts of aggression after watching televised violence. Whether they were so stimulated depended on social and personal factors. For example, an emphasis by parents on non-

[1] H. Himmelweit, A.N. Oppenheim, P. Vince, *Television and the Child*,' Oxford University Press, 1958, p. 20.
[2] Op. cit., p. 215.
[3] UNESCO, *The Influence of the Cinema on Children and Adolescents*, 1961.
[4] J.D. Halloran, R.L. Brown, D.C. Chaney, *Television and Delinquency*, Leicester University Press, 1970, p. 178.

aggression would reduce the impact, as would an easy pattern of communication within the family which allowed for self-expression. This report concluded that 'the mechanism of being incited to aggressive behaviour by seeing violent films shows up in the behaviour only of some children who were found in several experimental studies to be previously high in aggression'.[1] Evidence presented to another American National Commission on the causes and prevention of violence makes a similar point. For example, one expert concluded that 'the emotional needs of children produced the media habits' and that 'certain personality traits leads to a taste for violent media material, and that this material serves some sort of very ill-understood psychological function for children with certain maladjustments'.[2] The type of function might be to provide an escapist fantasy or to 'control' the environment. A British research worker found that children vulnerable to the influence of televised violence and likely to reproduce it were those with few interests of their own, from lower income families, and those with unsatisfied needs in their human relationships.[3]

The analysis of the type of children and young people likely to be most adversely affected by violent films poses the question whether it is desirable to censor films of violence in order to eliminate the possibility that maladjusted and deprived youngsters may be stimulated by them to acts of violence. Such a course would be difficult because of the unpredictable nature of individual response to specific

[1]'Television and Growing Up: the impact of televised violence', *Report to the Surgeon-General's Scientific Advisory Committee on Television and Social Behaviour*, U.S. Government Printing Office, 1972, p. 18.
[2]Evidence of J.T. Klapper, Director of CBS Office of Social Research in 'Violence and the Media', R.K. Baker and S.J. Ball. *Report to the National Commission on the Causes and Prevention of Violence*, Mass Media Hearings, Vol. 9A, December 1969.
[3]B.H. Kniverton, 'Televised Violence and the Vulnerable Child' in *'Proceedings of the Royal Society of Medicine*, Vol. 66, no. 11, November 1973.

scenes and contexts. Most education, social welfare, and mental health workers would take the view that the basic but long term remedy to the problems posed would be to reduce deprivation, stimulate more positive and rewarding interests, and help the young people to overcome their problems of human relationships.

If censorship is considered as a preventive measure, it would be necessary to consider how much and which kind of aggressive action in films need to be eliminated. Are Tom and Jerry cartoons to go, or cowboy and James Bond movies, all of which are ranked as family entertainment with 'U' and 'A' certificates? Are crime films to be cut out or only those in which the villains are shown (at least until the end) as successful? Should policemen be shown using violence and would that be more harmful than aggressive criminals? Is the very gory incident more likely to evoke aggression than a series of quick and conventional shootings? Here again the social scientists have tried to give some guidance. Two professors who gave evidence to the American National Commission on the causes and prevention of violence indicated from their research that the variables were all important. The type of violence shown, the context in which it is shown, the people using it, the consequences shown to follow all mattered, as did the circumstances in which the film was viewed and the emotional makeup of the people viewing.[1] Both these academics held the view that very gory scenes of violence provoked a reaction of shock and distaste which increased the inhibitions against violent aggression. Thus 'showing scenes of carnage may evoke horror and distaste in the observer, which may be upsetting, but may also inhibit aggression'.[2] When gory details were left out, the viewer's imagination was stimulated to imagine them. Experiments

[1] Evidence of Prof. L. Berkowitz, University of Wisconsin and Prof. P. Tannenbaum, Annenberg School of Communications in *Violence and the Media*, op.cit.
[2] Prof. Berkowitz, op. cit.

had also shown that the showing of negative consequences to violence on film, as, for example, a severely wounded person, would lower the likelihood of aggressive behaviour. On the other hand, 'When the aggression appears to be justified in some manner it instigates more rather than less aggressive behaviour'.[1] If these conclusions were taken as a basis of censorship policy, the results would indeed be interesting. We should expect to see an end to the 'good' sheriffs, police, or lone adventurers killing in vengeance the villains and transgressors. Casual aggression, fights, and shootings would have to go unless they were shown in bloody detail to result in the most heartrending suffering. Jokey killing of the James Bond variety could never be allowed.

Thus far, the immediate or short term effect of viewing violence in film has been considered. The other great cause for concern is said to be the long term effect repeated viewings have in causing people to become less sensitive to aggression and the suffering it causes and in accepting violence as an appropriate solution to personal and social problems. The behavioural scientists have little to offer in the form of evidence from experiments; we are back in the realm of social observation and speculation. Do films express social values, do they shape them or is there a process of interaction? Is violence in films an expression of our disturbed and fast changing society or does it help to feed the tendency to sudden change through violent means? Does the message that we receive justify aggression, and thus stimulate it, or does it show the disastrous consequence of such aggression?

We know that there is a strong demand for films showing violence. The film industry responds readily to demand and the run of the mill crime and war movies would not be produced unless they paid in terms of box office receipts. Long before films came into being, the nearest other art form, drama, showed equal preoccupation with violence

[1] Prof. Tannenbaum, op. cit.

and death. We are clearly concerned here with a continuing and long term need expressed over the ages. Is our own modern concern a result of the ready access and repetition of film viewing, or is it a reflection of our mid-twentieth century fear of the effects of human aggression which we have seen at Auschwitz, Hiroshima and Vietnam?

Whether we are capable of deadening and devaluing our response to the horrific results of violence is another aspect worth consideration. Experience during war shows that we can easily be conditioned to accepting death. At times of famine or disaster people quickly adapt themselves to the circumstances of suffering. The concentration camps produced values where survival was often only possible if the inmates disregarded the suffering of others. The conditioning of men and women not only to disregard the suffering of others but actively to inflict harm on them is another phenomenon which we are bound to accept. The casual brutality of soldiers as an occupying force is well known. That ordinary people may be conditioned into accepting and perpetrating torture must also be acknowledged. Recent experiments described in a Sunday newspaper[1] showed how a number of people in ordinary occupations could be persuaded into actively hurting a selected 'victim' if they were convinced that they were justified in so doing and were acting under legitimate authority. That indeed was the basis of the bureaucrat Eichmann's defence.

Human beings are clearly capable of being influenced into aggressive action by accepted leaders in positions of authority. Among the gamut of opinion leaders and authoritative figures which run from parents, teachers, political and religious leaders, army commanders to pop singer idols and peer group companions, films and film stars must have a place. It is likely that they portray and then reinforce to the viewer the contemporary views held in society. If John Wayne is shown in a hundred movies as

[1] *Sunday Times*, 19/5/74.

a good character who seeks the solution to social problems through violent action, that must reinforce the opinion that it is legitimate, even enviable, to tackle problems in such a way, although it does not directly lead many of us to adopt violence as a personal solution. If recent movies such as *Serpico* continue to show policemen as corrupt and violent in contrast to the genial, upright copper of the P.C. Dixon variety, or the tough but honest Barlow, we may receive and accept a message which is part of a contemporary disillusionment with figures of authority. A constant diet of TV films with free-shooting police such as *Starsky and Hutch*, *The Sweeney* and *Kojak* will lead us to accept violence by the agencies of law enforcement.

If films do have an impact on our attitudes towards violence by reinforcing and helping to legitimise certain opinions and actions, it is important to place that influence in a correct perspective. Films are only one of a series of messages that we receive constantly from personal and social as well as media sources. Why, then are they singled out so frequently to bear the responsibility for influencing antisocial actions? Why, for example, should James Cagney bear the blame more than Mickey Spillane's or Ian Fleming's heroes in books? The answer may lie in the earlier reference that was made to the power of films as an artistic medium. But while the shock effect of particular violent films may explain the call to ban them, it certainly does not provide a considered justification. The preceding analysis has shown that the most disturbing films are unlikely to be those which produce antisocial effects. If the violence in the films upsets us, it is likely to be stimulating our capacity to reject it, not to reproduce it. It is more likely to be undermining our resistances when we can laugh at it or easily accept it.

Hence an effort to censor violence from films which would reduce the risks of both imitation and 'desensitisation' of our resistance to actual violence would have to be directed in a very radical way. Repeated, casual violence, especially when carried out by socially acceptable figures, would have to be cut out while the most distressing sequences of suffering would be left in. Such a course of action would not be popular, least of all among the squeamish who protest against the shocking nature of violence in films that they have recently seen and those who call for tougher measures against crime. What would be the popular reaction to a censor who cut out Tom and Jerry, James Bond and the Sweeney but extolled *A Clockwork Orange* as a thoroughly moral film?

To summarise, the case for censoring violence in films rests on three different requirements. The first is to make the films acceptable to majority audiences and not to distress or frighten them excessively. The action necessary would be to cut down the number of violent films and those aspects of violence which are particularly distressing, such as rape, torture, or injury shown in close detail and violence towards children or other victim figures, especially where shown in a familiar context. The second justification for censorship rests on the need to prevent individuals already emotionally disturbed and pre-disposed to violence from being stimulated to acts of aggression. The necessary action would be to remove all violent acts by any characters with whom those individuals might identify; these would include all varieties of models such as soldiers, police, cowboys as well as gang leaders, villains, and robbers. The third argument for censorship of violence aims to strengthen the attitudes of normal well adjusted adults against accepting aggression and violence as part of socially acceptable action. There is, of course, a very big question as to whether violent action is sometimes an acceptable mode of behaviour, for example for self defence or in time of war. If that question is put aside and the need to condition adults against violence accepted, it would be necessary to eliminate all episodes of violence in films which were presented as legitimate, especially when performed by acceptable models such as war heroes, family men, crime fighters and police. It would also be useful to present any episodes of violence in a way which emphasised the suffering inflicted by violent action.

To take any of these aims on which to rest a policy and set of rules for censorship or movie making would present problems. It has earlier been shown that some degree of violent action is highly popular in films, especially when carried out by hero figures with whom we can identify. Yet the research evidence and the conclusions drawn emphasise that these episodes are the most likely to provide models for action and to encourage the acceptability of violence. The depiction of violation of the home environment and acute suffering would strengthen our defences against accepting violence, but to leave in, or put in, such episodes in films would be highly unpopular. Present censorship practice by the British Board of Film Censors appears to cut out both the number of violent episodes and the amount of explicit detail and suffering shown. While the Board's justification of its cuts is the need to curb violence as a possible model, its actual actions appear to be more directed to limiting public complaint and making the violence shown more acceptable. We are left in the odd situation that the unofficial censoring body which bases its case for continuing prior censorship on the violence content of films and the harm caused by that content to society, is not exercising its powers in such a way as to achieve those aims.

Lastly, the question must be asked why so much effort has and is continually being put into elaborate research studies which seek to associate screened and actual violence through causal links. If the objective is to discover ways of limiting violence in society, there are a good many other candidates for examination which would repay more attention. More examination of the way in which alcoholic consumption leads to aggressive action, for example, might lead to some startling conclusions. A recent review of studies which have been made on alcohol stated that 'an association between recent alcohol consumption, with presumably some degree of intoxication, and violent offences has been amply demonstrated.' It also made the point that 'surprisingly little is known about the relationship between drinking histories and criminal careers ... The remarkably few recent studies of samples of excessive drinkers or alcoholics have tended only to describe the association between drinking and convictions for drunkenness offences.'[1] If further research strengthened the association between alcohol and violent crime, a case for banning or restricting alcohol in order to prevent violence could be made. That such studies are not pursued suggests that the conclusion is one which we would not like to reach. In other words, nearly everyone enjoys drink and believes they can handle it. To see it banned because some people behave aggressively when drunk would not be popular, so we do not demand research which would seek to establish causal links.

The tendency to see bad influence in the screened image may, if it is not too fanciful, be compared with the obsession in the more distant past with magic and witchcraft. Our ancestors sought explanations for death and disaster much as we do and their preoccupation was with evil magic spells and their consequences. Perhaps our modern equivalent is the exploration through all our scientific techniques of the spell cast by the moving image on the screen and its imagined consequences. And just as magic spells meant witchhunting and witchburning, do we not seek to exorcise the magic of the screen image through excision and censorship?

To bring the argument down to earth again, our pursuit of screened violence in research studies is an effort to explain actual violence in society in a way which fits in with our dislike of some of the unpleasant images in films. There is, moreover, an over-emphasis on the influence of all the media which is based on the assumption that if only the depiction of violence could be stopped, actual

[1] J. Mott and T. Hope, 'Alcohol and Crime' in *Home Office Research Unit Bulletin*, No. 3, Spring 1976.

violence would end too. Such wishful thinking is both simplistic and unhelpful. Violence is a part of human life which causes us concern when it reaches intolerable levels. In medicine, fever is a symptom of illness but not its cause. Treatment of, for example, tuberculosis based only on the elimination of feverish symptoms rather than the healing of diseased lungs would be a palliative rather than a cure. Similarly the elimination of filmed violence will not cure the disease of actual aggression. Film is only a minor part of the whole gamut of attitude forming influences in our society and one which reflects our preoccupations. Art indeed copies nature and not nature art.

To argue thus does not exclude the case for controlling the content of violence which is based on the distress and offence caused to the consumer. As the President of the Motion Picture Association of America argued: 'My commonsense tells me that the depiction of extreme violence or anything in the extreme is simply offensive to normal sensibilities. I don't need a scientist to tell me that. Whether or not it causes juvenile or adult delinquency, it's just offensive, and I'm against it.'[1] But if the film makers trim their product to meet the demand of consumers for protection from distress, disgust, and offence, that is very far from the elaborate justifications put forward for a quasi-governmental censorship system.

[1] Jack Valenti in *Violence and the Media*, op. cit., p. 196.

7

THE CENSORS AND THEIR JUDGEMENTS

The network of institutions which have powers to censor films is extensive and pervasive. Before a film may be exhibited to the public it has to jump numerous hurdles. If it is a film made in another country, it may be stopped by the Department of Customs and Excise and banned from entering the country. Before being exhibited at any publicly licensed cinema, it must receive the licence of the local authority where the cinema is situated. If it is intended for network release, 368 local authority district councils may be involved. In order to receive a local authority licence, the film must either be seen and approved by local councillors or possess a certificate awarded by the British Board of Film Censors. Although local authorities cannot delegate their function of film licensing to the BBFC, in practice they rely on the Board's decisions for 99% of their own, and it is true to say that nearly all the films seen in public cinemas must be seen and approved by the BBFC in order to receive a local authority licence.

Even with a certificate and a licence, the censorship process is not complete. The exhibited film is still subject to laws which may enable the film to be seized and a prosecution brought against the cinema owner. Up to 1977, action could be taken either by any citizen or by the Attorney-General against a film on the basis of the common law forbidding an indecent exhibition. Or it was possible for the Director of Public Prosecutions to take action under common law against a cinema as a 'disorderly house' where an indecent exhibition is being held.[1] Other charges which could be brought were for publishing obscene films and conspiring to publish them. In the case of the film maker John Lindsay, the Director of Public Prosecutions initiated the first charge after the films had been acquitted under the second.[2] The Criminal Law Act (1977) abolished these laws in relation to films and has instead brought films under the Obscene Publications Act but without the right of private citizens to bring prosecutions.

Not all these powers have been exercised at any one time. The Customs authority and the 'disorderly houses' law have been chiefly used in relation to films shown in club cinemas which are not subject to local authority licensing regulations. It is expected that ordinary public cinemas will be regulated by the British Board of Film Censors working through local authority licensing powers. But it is important to remember that legal powers do exist and the Customs powers remain. They can and are brought into use whenever either the authorities or the vigilante groups find that the normal processes of control have failed to stop the exhibition of a film they consider should be stopped. Censorship of films is conducted in a gentlemanly quasi-democratic way provided it operates with restriction sufficient to satisfy them. When it does not, the process becomes rougher as the frantic urge to ban by whatever means takes over.

However, the gentler silk glove end of the censorship

---

[1] A disorderly house was defined at the Court of Criminal Appeal as 'a house conducted contrary to law and good order in that matters are performed or exhibited of such character that their performance or exhibition in a place of common resort a) amounts to an outrage of public decency or b) tends to corrupt or deprave or c) is otherwise calculated to injure the public interest so as to call for condemnation and punishment' (1962 R. v. Quinn & Bloom) in *Law Commission Report on Conspiracy & Criminal Law Reform*, 1976, para 329.

[2] 'Cleared films to be prosecuted' in *The Guardian*, 1/11/75. Mr Lindsay was however, not found guilty in July 1977.

business is conducted by the British Board of Film Censors and the local authorities, and it is worth examining how they carry out their tasks.

The British Board of Film Censors is a minute organisation exercising a great deal of repressive power. It consists of a President, a Secretary and four other examiners of whom three are currently women. The President has always been appointed by the Incorporated Association of Kinematograph Manufacturers which has been described as 'purely a group concerned with the manufacture of cinema technology'[1] whose interest in questions of censorship appears to be obscure. However, the process of appointment includes 'soundings' taken by the Home Office with the local authority associations and a joint committee of the film industry. The President's role varies according to the personality involved, but he is usually intended as a figure of eminence and respectability rather than as an active and regular participant in the Board's work. He is often called in to see films which the examiners feel are going to be particularly contentious. The current President, Lord Harlech, gave backing to his then Secretary Stephen Murphy when he was under attack by the cinema trade in 1972.[2] The Secretary is the key figure on the Board, appointed after open advertisement and extensive 'soundings' carried out by the Home Office with local authorities and possibly with other interest groups. In the case of the current appointee, James Ferman, GLC and other local goverment officers were invited to meet the candidate for discussions in order to get an impression of him and the appointing committee included local authority members as well as representatives of the trade.

The Secretary is both mouthpiece for the Board and initiator of its policies. He has to satisfy the cinema trade that he is not subjecting it to excessive criticism and the

[1] G. Phelps, *Film Censorship*, Victor Gollancz, 1975, p. 99.
[2] Ibid., p. 84.

puritan groups that he is not allowing sexual permissiveness. He has to show the film distributors that he is not curbing their profits by refusing or overly cutting their products or by denying them to wider audiences by classifying them only for adults. He has to placate the film makers who object to having their work chopped about and the film critics who may attack his action in savaging a film of artistic merit. In short, his life is not a happy one, sandwiched between vociferous pressure groups, enraged artists and critics, and a trade already in financial trouble listening anxiously for the ring of its cash registers. But, most important of all, and indeed necessary if he is to sustain his morale and withstand the whips and scorns of criticism, he has to justify his position to himself. That means evolving some coherent philosophy for prior censorship of films in a society which otherwise allows free expression in the media without the formal apparatus of prior censorship backed by government regulation. Past censors lived in times of great moral certainty, backed by élitist and authoritarian attitudes. No doubt Joseph Brooke Wilkinson, Secretary of the Board from 1912-48, or his President, G.A. Redford, found no difficulty in 1913 in objecting to films which showed 'indecorous dancing', 'indelicate sexual situations', 'scenes tending to disparage public characters and institutions', or 'native customs in foreign lands abhorrent to British ideas'; the list reflects the inhibitions and prejudices of the age. A summary of the types of material eliminated in 1926 actually groups subjects under headings religious, political, military, social, questions of sex, crime and cruelty.[1] Such frankness, particularly in listing political and social taboos, would not be manifest today.

After 1932, the Board ceased to publish annual reports because of the 'mischevious construction' placed upon 'isolated sentences ... by taking them out of their context'.[3]

[1] J. Trevelyan, *What the Censor Saw*, Michael Joseph, 1973, p. 31.
[2] J. Trevelyan, *What the Censor Saw*, op. cit., pp. 40-2.
[3] Ibid., p. 30.

Retiring hurt, the BBFC maintained this stance of silence until the present when more pointed and consistent criticism combined with a desire to justify its work has prompted the present Secretary of the Board to issue its opinions in the form of a monthly bulletin. The nervousness, however, remains. The early bulletins were stamped 'Confidential' until leaked and reported on in the press. They are still not available to the public and local licensing authorities must pay a charge of £50 per annum for them.

Throughout the post 1945 era, the tone of pronouncements on censorship has gradually changed. John Trevelyan, Secretary of the Board from 1958-71, may have started his career with the view that '... broadly speaking, the Board's aim is to exclude from public exhibition anything likely to impair the moral standards of the public, by extenuating vice or crime or by depreciating social standards, or anything likely to give offence to any reasonably minded members of the public'.[1] But he himself has described his work as one of steady liberalisation of the material allowed, particularly with regard to sex, and, by raising the age of admission to 'X' films to eighteen years, he hoped to make virtually all films permissible for an adult audience. By the time he retired, Trevelyan had come to the conclusion that 'the time has come when we should treat adults as adults, and let them choose whether they will see a film or not'.[2] Trevelyan's background before he came to film censorship was in educational administration. No doubt there he learned, as all good educators do, that people do not learn by being restricted in their access to knowledge but form their adult judgement by considering the evidence before them.

Stephen Murphy, Trevelyan's successor, held office as Secretary for only 4 years. He came to the job from a censorship background in both the ITA and BBC. He was

[1] D. Hill, 'The habit of censorship, in *Encounter*, July, 1960.
[2] J. Trevelyan, *What the Censor Saw*, op. cit., p. 114.

well aware that the area of his work for which he received most backing was the one which he regarded as worthless in absolute terms, namely, the banning or trimming of excessive sexual content. He once told me that he regarded his function with regard to sex in films as 'servicing' the needs and inhibitions of certain sections of the public. He did however hold strong views about the possible harm which he believed could be caused by violence in films, and felt very real justification in the work he did to cut violent film scenes. Murphy perhaps lacked the resilience and experience in public relations necessary for a job so much in the public eye and may have found the lack of appreciation for his work hard to take. He came into office as the 'backlash' of the Festival of Light gathered strength and was at the heart of the controversies about *Last Tango* and *A Clockwork Orange* which he defended. During the period of Murphy's stewardship, the Board's basic approach was said to be that it 'makes no claim to set itself up as a guardian of public morality. It seeks, rather, to reflect intelligent, contemporary public attitudes.'[1] At the same time, the Board was said to exert its powers to protect children, to 'watch for anything which might "deprave or corrupt" or have any undesirable influence or effect upon audiences' and 'to judge public taste and to protect audiences from material that would be greatly and gratuitously offensive to a large number of people'.[2]

The latest successor to the post of Secretary, James Ferman, is different again. He is an American by birth and education, who has worked on both television and film documentaries and plays. Ferman has a passionate belief in film censorship, declaring on his apointment 'I can conceive of no society that would not place some limits on what is permissible on the screen. There is an area in which we have a duty to keep aspects of the human subconscious at bay, a kind of duty to say 'This far and no further'. The

[1] G. Phelps, *Film Censorship*, op. cit., p. 114.
[2] G. Phelps, ibid., p. 111.

issue to me is where you draw the line, not whether you draw the line.'[1] Although not a psychologist by training, Ferman's approach is basically that of a mental health hygienist. He appears to feel that the dark or fantasy sides of human nature must not be explored, let alone indulged, but firmly contained within the boundaries of a balanced and acceptable lifestyle. His is the very modern fear, born of awareness of the terror and wickedness of the twentieth century, that evil will again run free. The prevention of the cinematic expression of violence appears to be his method of controlling it in our minds and thus hopefully in our actions. But essentially, his position differs little from the erstwhile guardians of public morality who hoped to block off immoral thoughts by forbidding their expression; it simply has a more modern cloak.

It is interesting to analyse the reasons for the censor's cuts and bans, made apparent in the censor's formal letters to local authorities when distributors appealed to them to seek a licence for a film, and in the monthly bulletins issued by the Board since 1975. Where bans or cuts were made in sex films, Murphy used frequently to justify them on the grounds that the sex shown was 'exploitative'. The meaning of exploitation in this sense seemed to be that the sex shown was there to exploit the sex urge and to arouse and titillate, rather than to contribute to any development of plot and character. Among objections specifically mentioned were 'unusual' sex positions, masturbation, lesbianism and male homosexuality, fellatio and cunnilingus. More generally, a film was often said to be unacceptable to current British standards or as adult entertainment or, simply, as being beyond anything that the Board had yet certificated. Ferman has continued to rely on unacceptability or what is described as the current consensus of community standards, as his test, though he appears to have dropped Murphy's theme that exploitation of sex

[1]'New Censor Feels That Film Industry Is Out Of Touch With Society' in *The Times*, 20/6/75.

material is a cause for banning. He does however fall back considerably for justification on the common law on indecency which in 1975 was held to apply to films. How this is to be interpreted remains as much of a mystery as what is acceptable to current community standards or British taste. We have a few hints when the Bulletins talk of dangerous perversions but do not define them. In other cases reference is made to regulating the productions of other cultures by the standards of our own, which leads to the mind-bending thought that certain sexual practices are just not British, a judgement with delightfully comic overtones. But, clearly, the censors do have a list of rules, and one of the younger ones was indiscreet enough to mention a few of them (and his own views on them) in 1974 when he said, 'The Board's stand on sex cuts was difficult to defend. It was largely guided by what was accepted at the time and to some extent magazines like Playboy were used as a barometer. If full frontal nudes did not draw a prosecution of a magazine, it was thought all right to have them on film. But there were rules on sex positions. It was considered all right for a man to be seen on top of a woman but any scene with a woman on top of a man was always out.'[1] (Women's movement adherents might draw their own conclusions from this last prohibition.)

The Board has now apparently relaxed a former standard to allow homosexual lovemaking, although by saying that it will apply the same limits or criteria that it applies to heterosexual love scenes, it appears likely to run into some technical problems of definition. If homosexual intercourse is now in, can the Board admit heterosexual sodomy, or is that still a perversion? Films which deal with homosexuality, however, still appear to require an 'X' category even if the treatment excludes explicit lovemaking.

Major objection is made to films which link sex and

[1] T. Kerpel 'Censorship is needed' in *Kilburn Times*, 6/12/74.

violence, including rape and sado-masochism, particularly where sado-masochism appears to be shown as pleasurable, acceptable and even glamorous. Jaeckins' *The Story of O* is particularly criticised as propaganda for the maltreatment of women, seductive in its advocacy of what the censor, letting himself go, describes as depravity, corruption, and perversion. Having myself seen *The Story of O* when it was submitted to (and rejected by) the GLC in 1976, I find it difficult to read half as much into it as the censor. Unlike the book of the same title by Pauline Réage which is an erotic and sensitive exploration of the masochistic side of women's sexuality, the film was just another sex formula film, with the additional titillation of some whipping scenes. It was made with a glossy surface, an exceptionally pretty actress and attractive photography, but was designed in the usual, and to me boring, way for exclusively male appeal. The glamourous and expensive backgrounds alone placed it well beyond the bounds of self identification and reality and into that area of male masturbation fantasy that most of these formula films are designed for. Can it be that Frenchmen all over Paris where the film is freely shown are re-enacting the film (at great expense, when one considers the high cost of ancient chateaux, serving wenches, etc. which the film includes) on their hapless womenfolk? It would be interesting to know if the censor's worst fears are born out in practice.

Returning to the general theme of violence, the exclusion of exploitative violence is high upon the list of the censor's bans. The definition of unacceptable violence appears to be that which, in the censor's view, invites the audience to identify with the aggressor. Such a justification for cuts would be more consistent if the Board were not freely passing such police epics as *Sweeney* where the audience can easily identify with ruthless and violent police action. Allowable violence is also variously described as restrained, not very bloody, or clean and fast, lacking slow motion agony and spurting blood. Yet much of the research evidence on violence suggests that it is the possibility of violence which does not have bloody, painful, or messy consequences which may provide the strongest encouragement to violent action.[1] A similar probably misplaced concern is shown in the treatment of a film including much distressing material, for example, *Savage Man, Savage Beast* where the issue is of particular interest because the sequences are documentary. Two sequences showing a man mauled to death by a lion and the mutilation and killing of Amazonian Indians were cut as objectionable on the grounds that the detail was prurient and invited the viewer to be a spectator to atrocity.[2] Although the censor's objections have a high moral tone it remains questionable whether truth can ever be described as prurient and we should be protected from its bare and crude impact. Were not the documentary films of concentration camps taken in 1945 or the extracts shown on television from the Nazi film on the Warsaw Ghetto the most powerful revelation of those atrocities which alerted people to their evil?

Possibly films which deal with disturbing social and political themes are only acceptable once the danger is felt to be past. The recent decision of the censor to reclassify for adolescent audiences without cuts *Rebel Without a Cause*, the popular James Dean movie of the 1950s which had previously been cut and made available only to adults, is a case in point. The film was cut and banned to teenagers because it was thought to sanction and thus encourage the anti-social and rebellious behaviour of the young hero, particularly against his father. Similar bouts of censorious adult panic banned Marlon Brando in *The Wild Ones* in the 1950s, *Panic in Needle Park* which dealt with drugs in 1971 and *Manson* in 1973 because the censor felt it had the appeal of an attractive but anti-social lifestyle.[3] Certainly

[1] See Chapter 6.
[2] The sequel to this story is that it has now been established that the lion episode was not a real one, but a reconstruction enacted by amateurs. The film has been re-entitled *Zumbalah*, and given a BBFC certificate.
[3] See Chapter 2.

the censor was happy to reclassify the James Dean saga in 1976, but if a modern version with a different message as challenging in the 1970s as the Dean film was in the 1950s were to appear, would the decision be any different? The record of banning films felt to have a disturbing and threatening social or political message has been a consistent one. In the 1930s, the Board banned *Battleship Potemkin* as pro-Soviet propaganda. *I Was a Captive of Nazi Germany, Free Thaelmann* and a *March of Time* film illustrating German war preparations were all turned down in order not to antagonise Hitler's regime. In the post-war period, the Board banned two East German films showing the alleged Nazi past of a West German mayor and a general, *Holiday on Sylt* and *Operation Teutonic Sword*, although in both cases, the individuals' reputations could have been protected by legal action for defamation and one of them, General Speidel, did in fact successfully take such action.

In the 1960s, a film based on recent events called *The Christine Keeler Story* was banned, no doubt because the involvement of a Cabinet minister in the actual affair made the film politically embarrassing. If direct political censorship is now less apparent, films with material felt to be disturbing to the existing social order are more likely to attack. Back in 1930 Lord Tyrrell, the then President of the BBFC, commented when *Night Patrol*, a film on the white slave trade in London, was banned that the film would discourage the girls which London sorely needed to fill domestic vacancies.[1] That may seem comic today. But nearly thirty years later, Arthur Watkins, the then Board Secretary, was to say of the project to turn Michael Croft's book *Spare the Rod* into a film, 'The moral deterioration of a teacher and conditions of indiscipline in the classroom are not fit subjects to show children of school age ... there will be riots in the classroom if we pass this film.'[2] The motive for banning always remains the same: the message is too

[1] D. Hill, 'The habit of censorship' in *Encounter*, July, 1960.
[2] Ibid.

disturbing and may undermine the existing social order, whether it concerns Croft's schoolboys, James Dean's rebellious son in *East of Eden*, Brando's leather-jacketed motor cyclists in *The Wild Ones*, Californian hippies in *Manson* or the *Clockwork Orange* 'droogs' (which the Board under Stephen Murphy did, to its credit, pass).

Lastly, the work of the Board in censoring films for exhibition to children is worth examination. Although this aspect of the Board's work is not generally challenged, the type of material cut and the categorising of admission by certain ages is more controversial. At present an 'AA' film excludes young people under 14 and an 'X' film those under 18. The muddle about age admission certainly adds to the burden placed on cinema staffs. If cashiers and ushers find it hard to distinguish between mature 16 and 18 year olds for an 'X' certificate admission, the problem of telling the difference between 13 and 14 year olds for an 'AA' certificate film is harder still, when variations in height and pubescent development are considerable at that age. Most recently the BBFC has suggested raising the minimum age for admission to 'AA' films to 16, on the grounds that more films could be made available within that category. Whether it is worth distinguishing films for the two year gap between 16 and 18 is questionable. It may be that the only worthwhile distinction is before and after the age of puberty.

The criteria used for censorship are puzzling if the censor's comments are taken as evidence and appear to rely more on what parents might find offensive than on what might frighten or distress children. Any coarse language, for example, evidently lifts a film immediately out of the blameless 'U' category into the parental warning 'A' category, or even into the 'AA' category for 14 years and over, although the film (as in the case of an Australian sheep shearing saga called *Sunday Too Far Away*) may be said by the censor to have visual material of a 'U' character. Sexual activity is felt to be an obvious reason for banning films to children below puberty. Even a filmed sequence when a bull mounts a cow was felt in one case to put a film beyond the desirable limits for the under 14s. The latest of the *Carry on* films (*Carry on, England*) was said to have crossed the boundary from 'A' to 'AA' classification and taken itself out of the class of family entertainment because of the exhibition of women's bare breasts in relative close up in one of the comic scenes. Alas, it appears that actual nudity can never be permitted to the under fourteens, who have lived for many happy years on the coarse humour and sexual innuendo of the numerous earlier *Carry On* sagas. Innuendo, titillation, and humour with the overtones that sex is naughty is, it seems, so much more acceptable than the actual and dangerous sight of women's breasts. Six months later, the censor reported that he had been able to re-classify *Carry On, England* as an 'A' film after the sight of those breasts had been reduced to a long shot in the film. But where does the real prurience lie, in the sequences mentioned or in the censorship judgements made? As far as violence is concerned, the Board's policy appears to be to cut for exhibition to the under 14s any violence which is distressing in its detail. Although this judgement is acceptable, it avoids the question as to whether repeated enjoyable violence is desirable in films for children. There is also the question of films which are frightening without being violent, bearing in mind a young child's inability to distinguish fantasy from reality. My own childhood memories, for example, are of being more terrified by Disney fantasies of violence in *Pinocchio* and *Snow White* than by any ordinary adventure film. This is a difficult area to fathom and more expert advice is probably needed to lay down suitable guidelines for the Board's use so that the children's needs and not their parents' fears or inhibitions are the proper subject of the control exercised.

In all its work, the Board always defends itself against accusations of being a private organisation responsible to no one by referring to the role of the local authorities as censorship bodies. The Board likes to point out that it is up to local authorities to validate its judgements and that they may vary its certificates either by licensing material that the Board has banned or by banning films which the Board has certificated. It is claimed that local authority participation in censorship provides an appeal procedure and a democratic element in the process which also allows for what are described as regional variations in taste. In recent months, the Board has tended to pass more decisions on to local authorities, especially where films of artistic merit are concerned. Both *Texas Chain Saw Massacre* and Pasolini's *Salo* were passed to the GLC for decision after a national certificate had been refused and without attempts at cutting; the first was passed by the GLC and the second refused. If local authority decisions on films are to be taken as an example of democratic choice, it is important to examine the way in which they carry out their censorship function to see if the claims for democracy in censorship can be justified.

Of all the local authorities exercising censorship powers, the Greater London Council is the most important because it has the largest numbers of cinemas within its area. The GLC operates through its Film Viewing Board, which, up to 1977, was a sub-committee of its Arts and Recreation Committee, on the curious assumption that censorship has something to do with art. The Board consists of twenty members, not necessarily members of the parent committee, serving in numbers relative to the strength of the political parties but otherwise self-selected, with the Chairman and Vice Chairman of the Arts and Recreation Committee as ex-officio members. Attendance at film viewing sessions varies; the quorum is five and the usual attendance is around the half way mark. It used to amuse me when journalists or film critics tried to read some kind of consistent thinking into the Board's decisions to pass or reject particular films. The only decisive factor governing the decisions was who had turned up to a particular viewing session.

General attitudes were well established from the censorious who voted against everything to the anti-censorship councillors who were determined to provide an antidote to them. The number of considered thinkers in the middle who might vote either way were in a minority. Board decisions on films were never taken on a party basis, but it is true to say that Conservatives were more usually among the 'no' voters and Labour provided the bulk of the 'yes' votes. Whether this reflected age (Labour members in my time on the Board were generally younger), ideology, or solidarity with colleagues is hard to say, possibly a little of each. The GLC concerned itself with films or parts of films banned by the BBFC or with classifications against which the distributors were appealing. Although it could not delegate its responsibility to the BBFC, the Council always refused to review films passed by the Board with a view to banning them. It came closest to so doing in 1972/73 when the Film Viewing Board actually saw *A Clockwork Orange* (but took no action on it) and when a motion put forward by Councillor Frank Smith to review *Last Tango* was debated by the full Council but turned down.

Although the Film Viewing Board's members must have viewed a film before they vote on it, the same is not true for members of the full Council if they are called upon to vote. One fourth of the Board's members present when the decision was taken or any eight members of the Council may requisition the Board's decision to the superior Committee and from there to the full Council for a final decision. In such circumstances, the Council has been notable for reversing the decisions of the Board, with a good half of the members voting without having seen the film. I well remember one elderly colleague telling me that it was beneath his dignity to have seen a particular film as he proceeded to vote against a licence for it.

Censorship at the GLC is reasonably well organised and confined to the Council's members. Elsewhere in the country, however, the position may be very different with the police playing a surprisingly prominent part. When the GLC took evidence from representatives of local authorities on film censorship, we were told that in both Manchester and Barnsley the Chief Constable of Police would take the initiative in referring films to the local authority for consideration. They were mostly films which had a BBFC certificate but which had received notorious press publicity. One of the Councillors told us that they rarely felt able to pass a film referred at the Chief Constable's request for fear of being labelled as part of the 'dirty raincoat' brigade. Films in Manchester may also be reviewed at the request of a licensing officer or any member of the appropriate committee, and decisions must be confirmed by the full Council. Other local authorities, such as Wirral, were said to refer films to the Magistrates for a decision on licensing, a far remove from the 'democratic' element lauded by the BBFC.

A few Councils make more systematic attempts to review films. Berkshire has a County Viewing Committee acting for all its county districts except Reading. Recently, at the request of a single local resident, that Committee decided to ban *Emannuelle II*, which had been granted a BBFC certificate, from all its cinemas. Southend Council decided in 1971 that it would review all 'X' films and for eight months actually did so, until pressure of time (and probably excessive weariness) brought about a change of mind.[1] Stafford Council had a Film Preview Subcommittee which originally decided to see all 'X' films but later decided to call in for review films on a blacklist which it compiled. A list of thirty-odd films issued in October 1975 was based on the synopses primarily derived from the trade paper *Screen International*.[2] Stafford's Committee tried to ban the Town Hall's booking by a bona fide film society intending to show two films on its blacklist. However, this decision was overturned by the full Council and resulted in the abolition of the Preview Committee.

The general attitude of councillors towards local authority censorship is one of indifference and embarrassment at

[1] G. Phelps, *Film Censorship*, op. cit., p. 182-3.
[2] P. Hames, 'Censorship – Stafford Style' in *Film* (Journal of the BFFS), February, 1976, No. 34.

having to deal with the subject at all. With the exception of a very few councillors who see themselves as the guardians of decency and public morality, and who largely staff the film preview committees, the majority dislike the role of local authorities, feel that they are unqualified to act as censors and shrink from any involvement in matters to do with 'pornography'. The elaborate theory of the BBFC that its decisions are largely acceptable to local authorities and thus attain the seal of local democratic approval is far from the truth. It is the reluctance of local councillors to become involved in a distasteful job which they feel to be outside their true role in running local services which is the real bedrock of local government complaisance in the film censorship system.

Mention has been briefly made of the role of the police in areas outside London. Within the London area, the police made no attempt to initiate action with regard to films shown at licensed cinemas during my involvement at the GLC. Indeed, interviewed by us, two very senior Metropolitan Police officers professed, as personal opinions, a healthy scepticism about films' ability to provoke depraved or violent conduct. Boredom they thought appeared to be the most marked public reaction to 'pornographic' films, and the films most likely to cause violent reactions in the audience were concerned with rock music rather than crime or violence. The police do, however, enter the picture when a complaint against a film by a member of the public is referred by the Attorney General to the Director of Public Prosecutions, who then asks the police to investigate both the film and the audience reactions. The police then become the censors together with the Director of Public Prosecutions because it is on the former's advice and the latter's decision that a prosecution is initiated in the Courts. Such was the procedure followed in the case of *More About the Language of Love*.

If the police are thought to be less than qualified as film censors, what can be said about Customs Officers, who have several times been brought into play as a censorship body to prevent films from even being considered by the official censorship bodies. Under the Customs Consolidation Act of 1876, indecent or obscene articles may not be imported into the country. In two recent instances, this power has been used to prevent films from being considered at all in Britain. In one case, the film *Deep Throat* was to be shown to an invited audience in London as part of a bipartisan discussion on censorship. The action of Mary Whitehouse in pressing the Customs to ban its importation for that purpose shows how unwilling she and her kind are to see open debate of the issues involved.[1] The second instance concerns the Japanese masterpiece, Nagisa Oshima's *Empire of the Senses*, which was shown at the London Film Festival in 1976 and was awarded the British Film Award of 1976 as 'the most original and imaginative film shown at the National Film Theatre during the year'. Even before the film received rave reviews by film critics, the Customs department became active. The film had been brought into Britain under a special arrangement which operates between Customs and the National Film Theatre for the Festival. Customs wrote to insist that it must be sent directly out again, or if anyone else wished to import it for showing, it should be returned to Customs who would then decide whether it was decent enough to enter the country officially. The cordon sanitaire could otherwise not be breached.

There is no doubt that in their desperation to prevent films they consider obscene from being shown, the agents of repression are ready to take more and more extreme action. In the case of the film which the Dane Jens Jorgen Thorsen was said to be planning to make in Britain on the sex life of Jesus Christ, appeals were made to the Home Secretary to ban Mr Thorsen from entering the country. The Archbishop of Canterbury threatened to invoke the blasphemy law if the film were ever made, the Archbishop of Westminster urged backers not to finance it and Equity

[1] See Chapter 3 p. 48-9.

members not to act in it. Violence to Mr Thorsen was threatened by a Conservative party agent should he appear in Britain, and even the Queen's alleged opinion was dragged into the matter by the Prime Minister. It took the Bishop of Wakefield to draw the conclusion that demands for a ban on the entry of Mr Thorsen to Britain would be 'first steps towards authoritarianism which would in the end take away from us that freedom of choice which is essential for the development of character',[1] adding that there was nothing Mr Thorsen could do that would diminish the majesty and power of Christ. When Thorsen arrived in Britain in February 1977 to promote another of his films, he was refused admission on the grounds that his presence might provoke demonstrations and was not conducive to the public good. Even the presence of a Danish maker of sex films was felt to be a danger to the British people.

This last ridiculous example is an illustration of the link between the harsh forms of true authoritarianism and the censorship system. Provided the habitual silk glove method works, it is allowed to do so. But it is there under sufferance. If it does not work to the satisfaction of the censorious, no one should underestimate its links with the government operated repression of cruder authoritarian regimes of which indeed it is the softer but still repressive representative. And while the Government is always careful to distance itself from the usual censorship process, its agents in the form of police, customs and immigration officers, and the Director of Public Prosecutions are there to provide state power when easier methods fail.

[1] *Evening Standard*, 16/9/76.

8

CONCLUSIONS:
DO WE NEED PATERNALISTIC CONTROL?

During the eight years 1968-75, nearly 4,000 feature films were submitted to the British Board of Film Censors for certification. Over one third did not receive their certificates until they had had a varying amount of material cut out. Over half the 'X' films, themselves representing nearly half of all films certificated, were cut before certification. 181 films were banned entirely, representing 7% of all 'X' films or 4% of all films submitted in the period, although 51 of these were later certificated after the cuts demanded had been made. The numbers of films cut and placed in each category remained steady from year to year during the period. The significance of these figures is startling. Putting aside films censored for children's viewing, the Board did not allow the adult public to see over half the films intended for adult consumption until cuts had been made. And these figures do not include the traditional male-oriented sex movies designed for the club circuit which do not require prior censorship. Suppose half the books intended for adult reading were cut before permission to print was given, or half the plays before they could be put on? Would such a situation ever be tolerated?

The question which must be asked is why prior censorship of films enforced on the cinema going public is still accepted in Britain. Is the medium of film such as to warrant separate treatment? Some may argue that films shown in cinemas are different from plays shown in theatres, both as regards the quality of the product and the type of audience. Perhaps the comparison adverse to the film could be made in the early days of cinema when both

127

techniques and content were crude, but it would be difficult to argue today that film is inferior to live performance as an artistic medium. Again, when cinemas stood on every suburban shopping street for bi-weekly visiting, the élitist argument that the family entertainment of the masses required control had more substance if not justification. Today film going is a minority recreation most popular among the young adult group. Prices of admission are comparable with the least expensive theatre seats. The number of publicly licensed cinema screens in Greater London was 234, compared with some 85 professional theatres in 1976, and cinema attendances for Great Britain in 1975 were 116 millions compared with 37 millions at the theatre.[1] Visits to the cinema are today much more a question of planned recreation closely analogous to buying a book or visiting the theatre than they ever were before. It is television which, censored under the heading of 'programme control', provides the family entertainment directly into our homes.

Looking at the stated aims of the British Board of Film Censors – to protect children, to exclude what could have an undesirable influence or effect on audiences, and to protect audiences from gross offence – we can accept the aim of protecting children although the extent and way in which it is done are open to discussion. The question of harm or undesirable influence has, however, been examined at some length in preceding chapters. Analysis of the best research evidence available shows that explicit sexual material has not been shown to cause viewers to behave in any anti-social way and the most that can be said on effect is that sex films lead, as they are intended to, to sexual arousal. It is not a crime to be sexually stimulated nor can it be shown to harm the person so stimulated. If men seek to identify and fantasize in films where the man is the all powerful, dominating male brute, that may be a

[1] Statistics drawn from the Business Monitor of the Department of Industry and from the Theatres Advisory Council.

false stereotype which diminishes both his own and his partner's true sexuality, but it is unfortunately common in less as well as more explicitly sexual films. Probably the men who seek out films of this nature are compensating in their fantasies for a less than dominating actual relationship with their real life spouses or girl friends. 'Me Tarzan, you Jane' is a hard role to sustain in real life.

That violence on film leads to violent action is readily assumed but not at all proven. It is easy to conclude that because the press reports an attack following the pattern of a crime seen in a film that the one inspired the other. *A Clockwork Orange* was particularly subject to this kind of popular journalistic attack, for example, by David Holbrook who in a letter to *The Times* quoted several 1974 Australian press reports of crimes as 'evidence' of the connection between the film and crimes committed.[1] On two occasions, I noted medically qualified people making the same kind of point and took the trouble to follow their allegations up. In one instance, a Dr Schmideberg, editor of the *International Journal of Offender Therapy* alleged in an article that the film 'has been shown directly in several cases in England to have been a motive force in turning a young person to assault and murder'.[2] When questioned, the doctor referred me as evidence of her assertion to four newspaper reports in the course of 1973 where youths were reported to have beaten up and in two cases killed people in a fashion alleged to have been patterned on the film incidents. In her letter to me she owned that it was not possible to prove or disprove the statement she had made with such conviction, but added her personal opinion that suggestion was a powerful spur to action. In the second instance, Dr I. H. Mills, a Professor of Medicine at Cambridge University wrote to *The Times* alleging that 'In a number of court cases it has been revealed that a violent

[1] Letter to *The Times* from D. Holbrook, 8/10/76.
[2] See P. Evans, 'Boy Killer exalts power of a minor' in *The Times*, 21/1/74.

sex crime followed an obsession with reading such material. Anyone who suggested that there should be limited availability to the general public of material portraying infliction of pain in association with sexual activity would I think have good grounds for making the suggestion'.[1] Again when I wrote to him to discover the source of his data, the Professor replied that he had no current data on the cases where someone accused of a sex crime had been known to be reading books on violence and sex but had made a mental note when those cases were reported in the press. The casualness with which assertions are made of a connection between reported crime and films (or in the second case books) of violence is staggering. A moment's reflection on press practice should yield the thought that journalists like to make their writing colourful by turning a gang assault into a 'Clockwork Orange' crime. Moreover, crimes noted and commented on in the press are only a tiny proportion of all crimes of violence and provide no firm statistical basis for analysis. But it appears that even highly trained professional people are prepared to accept anecdotal material without any other substantiation or evidence and to draw the conclusion that a press report on, say, a so-called 'Clockwork Orange' crime means that the crime was caused by the film. The press is equally guilty of sensationalising crime reports.

It is, of course, tempting to find so easy and direct an explanation of violent crime, one that makes the solution so easy too. Just ban the films and the crime will go away. But even before we look at the copious research evidence, a little questioning will sow doubts: from where did Jack the Ripper draw his inspiration or for that matter Bluebeard or the Borgias if films were not available? The evidence on violence cites a multiplicity of factors including material and cultural deprivation, poor family relationships, and unsatisfied emotional and human relationships among the causes of violence. While research indicates that a few

[1]Letter to *The Times* from Dr I.H. Mills, 23/8/76.

people predisposed to violence and emotionally disturbed may be stimulated to acts of violence by books or films, to what extent can we expect by eliminating specific stimuli to sidetrack the explosion in their flawed temperaments? How much violence would need to be eliminated to achieve such a purpose? Would the public, for example, be prepared for the elimination of all fist fights, murders, shoot-outs at the O.K. corral in order to achieve the possible objective of not provoking a tiny handful of disturbed persons to actual assault?

Looking at another aspect of the violence question, the possibility that we are habituated to accepting violence by seeing it portrayed on film, it is very likely that the 'cleanest', easiest violence may be the most corrupting. Mary Whitehouse, curiously enough, also drew this conclusion in another context when she feared that uncensored documentary film of war would so repel viewers that it would sap the national will to wage war.[1] The same point was made in *A Clockwork Orange* when the hero was brainwashed *against* violence by being forced to watch endless horrific enactments of it as aversion therapy. Would we as a society be prepared to see violence on film only in the most sickening and heartrending detail in order to achieve the possible objective of inoculating ourselves as normal, healthy people against the idea that violence is desirable and pleasurable and has no consequences?

The evidence on 'harm' caused by film is, therefore, of limited significance as a prop to censorship. Where, after elaborate investigation, film could be shown to have some contributory effect on action, there are so many qualifying factors about the context, the surroundings, and the individual's emotional make up and state of mind that the conclusion must be that in a society full of different stimuli of all kinds, the isolation of film for separate and invidious treatment is not justified. Far stronger evidence might well

[1] *Guardian*, 6/4/76.

131

be drawn for, say, the harmful effects of alcohol leading to violent behaviour.[1] Of the mass murderer William Hughes, for example, his sister said that 'drink was his big downfall. After a drink he would be capable of hitting anyone who looked at him twice.'[2] Among forms of entertainment, boxing and wrestling are both clear examples of violent action which can easily be copied and involve enthusiastic vocally aggressive participation by the audience. Violence at and following football matches provide a stronger case for banning than films, as numerous incidents of 'soccer hooliganism' testify, but we do not suggest stopping the pleasure of countless fans in order to prevent the violence.

If we turn to the question of protection against offence, there cannot be the same dependence on a tone of earnest morality for censorship justification. The wish not to be upset or offended can be accepted and possibly catered for. It is highly undesirable, however, to force some people's low level of shockability onto others by the compulsory means of censorship. If old Mr and Mrs Bloggs would be shocked by a film showing at their local cinema, why should young Joe Bloggs their grandson have to suffer limitations on his entertainment because of their suscepti-bilities? The censors of course seek to find a consensus of acceptability in the standards they apply, but that is an impossible task in view of variations in taste arising from age, family upbringing, religious beliefs and other factors, and the very individual way people 'read' and react to films. What shocks and upsets one person is a matter of indifference to another. Moreover, in such an exercise, there is a tendency to yield ground to those who make the most vehement objections and it is very plain that the sexually puritan groups make themselves strongly felt, bolstered up by ample press publicity. The film director Michael Winner quoted the censor Stephen Murphy as

[1] See pp. 105-6.
[2] J. Swain, 'The Violent Life of a Slum Child' in *Sunday Times*, 16/1/77.

saying 'You keep attacking me but if it wasn't for me things would be worse. I'm fending off the Festival of Light by giving into them a little.'[1]

What evidence we have from public opinion surveys shows that people are less shockable than might be supposed about sex. For example, the only manifestation chosen from a list thought by over half a sample surveyed to be 'pornographic' was a live performance on stage of the sex act.[2] Only 8% of another sample said they had ever been seriously upset by indecency in a film.[3] It is a great deal more likely that box office receipts tell the true story; as the managing director of EMI, Bob Webster, put it 'The only truly national taste is for films like *Emmanuelle*. Everybody likes sex.'[4] Yet the elaborate farrago of censoring sex from films remains, complete with lists of 'perversions', forbidden positions in the sex act, and close-up shots of particular activities, and is pressed on the public in a compulsory system.

There is an important sense too in which the cuts in violent scenes also seek to reduce shock and offence. Violence in films appears to worry people even more than sex; 66% in a public opinion survey in 1972 thought that violence was the more serious worry in TV and films as against 11% who chose sex.[5] As it is unproven that the connection between violence in films and social harm is a causal one, the case for cutting violence must rest equally with sex on the desire to prevent distress and offence.

The wish of the cinema trade to protect itself from criticism, even when that criticism is violent and ill-informed, may also be a legitimate aim. It was, indeed, a prime reason for the setting up of the British Board of Film Censors in 1912 as a voluntary trade body. What is

[1] L. Richmond, 'How To Make Movies Without Upsetting the Censor' in *Forum*, March, 1976, vol, No. 1.
[2] G. Phelps, *Film Censorship*, op. cit., p. 228.
[3] See Chapter 3, p.45.
[4] M. Pye, 'The Man Behind Your Movies' in *Sunday Times Magazine*, 23/3/76.
[5] G. Phelps, *Film Censorship*, op. cit., p. 227.

increasingly open to question is whether the trade's wish to protect itself from criticism and from legal actions justifies the panoply of compulsion and government backed censorship powers.

My own objection to compulsory prior censorship is threefold. First, it is an authoritarian act of formal political repression in a largely free society. Second, it is a manifestation of paternalism. Third, it is a diminution of the individual's freedom to think, judge, and choose for himself.

Censorship is a politically authoritarian act because it seeks to control and restrict the content and style of the message which a film conveys to an audience. Films are not just a product for entertainment or even for the appreciation of some ethereal 'artistic' qualities. All art, entertainment and cultural artefacts contain messages and it is those messages that either reinforce our social and political values or introduce discordant ideas disruptive to the status quo. In other words, 'Politics concerns the distribution of resources, power and prestige in society, and culture plays a part in determining that distribution because it is transmitted by institutions which are part of society and because it provides people with symbols, myths, values and information about their society ... Consequently, the decision as to what will be shown on the screen must inevitably be political, involving considerations that go beyond the merit of the cultural product in question.'[1] Very frequently, the censorship is exercised in favour of the older, more conservative groups in society who fear the eruption of the young across the generation gap; the censorship of films showing youthful rebellion (James Dean, Marlon Brando, etc.) and of sexually explicit material more acceptable to young people than their elders are both examples of the point in question. The language of censorship also provides

[1]H. J. Gans, 'The Politics of Culture in America' (1969) in D. McQuail (ed.) *The Sociology of Mass Communications*, Penguin, 1972, p. 373.

ominous signs of Orwellian thought control. Not only the Festival of Light use the phrase 'quality control' to describe censorship; it is also to be found in the BBFC's recent bulletins. The expression 'acceptable adult entertainment' is another one used by the censor which prompts the very pertinent question 'acceptable to whom?', and for that matter on what possible basis or justification is the acceptability founded?

The authoritarian nature of censorship is also to be found in the outbursts of some of its adherents. Mervyn Stockwood, Bishop of Southwark, was moved to write an article in which he praised the communist governments of Eastern Europe for cleaning up pornography – 'Those of us who have visited socialist countries in Europe know that if a communist government were to be established in Britain, the West End would be cleaned up overnight and the ugly features of our permissive society changed within a matter of days.' The Bishop's praise of autocratic action in communist countries to remove the outer manifestations of pornography put the establishment forces in Britain in some dilemma. Permissiveness has always been attributed by conservatives to left wing corruption of our traditional values. But even *The Times* which has thundered in furious campaigns against pornography had to see the connection when its leaders wrote of the Bishop 'In short for the sake of closing down a few cinemas and bookshops in the West End, we should be prepared in his view to accept the total censorship of the mind, and of religious thought and practice, which is characteristic of Marxist societies.'[1] The link between censorship and authoritarian attitudes can also be seen on the right in Mary Whitehouse's fear that uncensored films and television showing the horrors of war might so sicken people that they would no longer be ready to fight. Censorship is here seen as an aid to military endeavour.

Both these viewpoints are of interest because they show

[1]'Sad, Silly and Wrong' in *The Times*, 1/11/75.

the close links between censorship and political repression. We should not really need reminding of that particular connection. The most autocratic societies politically are always those which exercise the strongest censorship of the media and the arts, whether they are regimes of the right or left. Stalinist Russia and Nazi Germany were both models in this respect, dealing harshly with both sex and violence in entertainment. Would anyone dare say that those societies were healthier and less violent, let alone more just to their citizens? Coming closer to home, can we really find Victorian society with its strictly observed appearances and inhibitions an era of moral sexual behaviour when child prostitution was allowed to flourish?

My second objection to censorship is that it is paternalistic. During the course of our GLC examination of film censorship, the viewpoint put to us by the Church of England Board of Social Responsibility[1] was that the mature members of society have a responsibility to protect not only children but the immature of all ages from possible harm. They thought that scenes of horror and violence in films, or those combining sex and violence might harm the immature and the sick. They also suggested that the uncontrolled display of violence might lead to the changed character of our society's way of life, freer but perhaps more callous. The Church of England Board's view that there are mature members of society who should protect the immature probably stems from the church concept of pastoral care. Such a concept has merit if we consider that every one of us has a duty to care for and be concerned with the welfare of our fellow citizens. The point that sticks in the throat, however, is why some of us are to be deemed immature and in need of protection while others are given the job of protecting us whether we like it or not. At a time of universal suffrage when every adult man and woman is thought fit to decide on the

[1]GLC Report, 26/11/74 (Exercise of the Council's powers of film censorship for adults).

government of the country, it is much harder to argue that at the same time we need protection from exercising similar decisions as to the type of film we should see. It is also worth pointing out that censors have no monopoly of insight and wisdom, and the state of scientific knowledge about what we might need protecting from is not such as to inspire confident and well based decisions. Perhaps acceptance of the concept of protection depends on whether you see yourself as a protector – knowledgeable, benign, disinterested and compassionate – or as one of those who is compulsorily to be protected. It is likely that those favouring censorship do not see themselves at the receiving end of the process.

The argument against paternalism was put eloquently by the late Bishop of Durham, Ian Ramsey, when he said 'But the major argument against censorship is that it infringes personality and liberty and encourages that kind of paternalism which can so easily degenerate into a patronising and self-righteous condenscension. The problem of censorship is indeed one version of the problem of paternalism. Most men would assume the 'natural right' of an adult to have access to all available information. The burden of proof, therefore, lies on the withholder to show why this information is not to be disseminated, or to be restricted ...'[1] Dr Ramsey argued further that every society needed a basic commitment towards some acknowledged symbols, some understanding of 'sacred' objects and of a special vision of society's future. His view was that 'the Christian's main concern must be to foster and to possess such a vision. With it the need for censorship will be severely reduced; without it censorship is an intolerable affront to personality, a suppression of personal freedom.'[2] The Bishop's view again draws attention to the problem of an acceptable consensus in a free and plural society. Is there today at a time of such swift and sometimes disruptive

[1] Ian Ramsey, 'Censorship' in *Crucible*, January, 1974, p. 8.
[2] Ibid., p. 12.

change an understanding on social mores sufficient to warrant censorship? The reality is that paternalistic concern is a cloak for the enforcement of minority establishment views on ordinary people who are quite as capable of making their own judgements.

Finally, if we accept that compulsory prior censorship of films is an unwarranted infringement on individual liberty, it is necessary to ask what system, if any, should replace it. The first principle should surely be that if any material in films is to be censored by force of law, the powers to do so and the offences should be set out by statute, and the trial should take place in open court where the decision should be taken by a jury. Such a process is normally applied in our society to areas where an 'offence' is said to have been committed, and it is the process by which both the theatre and printed publications may be brought to trial. The major difficulty in the operation of the present laws which control theatre and books lies in the problem of definition of offence. While there is a reasonable degree of understanding in the interpretation of the Race Relations Acts on what constitutes incitement to race hatred, the major statute controlling charges of obscenity is a very different matter. A reasonably certain definition of obscenity has never yet been made. That embodied in the Obscene Publications Acts of 1959 and 1964 and the Theatres Act of 1968 is the Hicklin judgement that the effect of the offending article has a tendency to 'deprave and corrupt' persons reading, seeing or hearing it. Yet the interpretation of 'deprave and corrupt' is full of pitfalls, and the recent decision of the Law Lords[1] to exclude expert medical evidence on whether the material on trial could be for the public good throws a jury back largely on its own emotional resources. Numerous attempts have been made to try and tighten the definition to assist the courts and for that matter the producers and publishers of books. Longford's Committee wanted a definition of 'outrage to

[1] R. v. Staniforth & R. v. Jordan, March, 1976.

contemporary standards of decency or humanity accepted by the public at large'. The Society of Conservative Lawyers included affront to contemporary standards of decency, and whether the dominant theme of the material 'appeals to a lewd or filthy interest in sex or is repellent'.[1] The Arts Council Working Party set up in 1968 to see if the obscenity laws could be improved went more deeply into the question of whether obscenity did corrupt at all and came to the conclusion that, since there was no incontrovertible evidence that it did, the law had best leave it alone. It recommended that the Obscenity Acts be repealed. On the other hand, the Law Commission in 1976 felt sufficient confidence in the 1959 Act to recommend that it be extended to include films and that various common law offences on public morals and indecency be repealed,[2] and that solution which is clearly the most equitable for films in relation to the other media has now been adopted in the Criminal Law Act 1977.

It is not intended here to reach final conclusions on whether or not society requires any protection at all against 'obscenity', violence or anything else in the media. My own opinion at this stage is that it is hard to justify criminal prosecution for providing entertainment which may offend but does not harm. A crime should have a victim. The introduction of a legal offence in the case of violence would be extremely difficult in view of the inconclusive evidence on what might cause harm and to which audiences. But what is indisputably important is that if there is to be an offence, it should be defined in law and should be made as clear and unambiguous as possible. So much is important and fair both for film makers and exhibitors and for juries.

The definition of legal offence does not however deal with two other problems, one concerning the overall

[1] Society of Conservative Lawyers, 'The Pollution of the Mind' quoted in National Council for Civil Liberties, *Against Censorship*, 1972, p. 31.
[2] *Report of The Law Commission on Conspiracy and Criminal Law Reform*, No. 76, 1976, H.M.S.O., p. 103 and p. 121.

standard of film content and the other the protection from shock and distress of those who do not wish to see certain kinds of film material. The Annan Committee on broadcasting thought that 'All societies have a notion of public decency ... However much notions of public decency have changed, a society which had lost all sense of differentiating between private and public behaviour would be a society which had lost all sense of human personality or sensitivity to what others feel.'[1] It felt that broadcasters had a case to answer on public decency as well as on the glorification of violence although it did not say what standards should apply. But the Committee's report rejected a proposal for a Broadcasting Council to adjudicate on 'offensive' programmes, placing the responsibility onto the BBC and IBA directly. Public regulatory corporations do not, of course, exist for the other media but the creation of a public advisory council on films might serve to intervene between the public and the direct commercial interest of exhibitors and distributors by bringing an informed body of opinion to bear on their operations and by reviewing films and assessing their impact. It could provide a channel of communication with the public where at present there is none apart from box office receipts and sensational press reporting.

The desire to protect people from offence is legitimate though the measures taken should not in my view be such as to restrict the liberty of other adult members of the public. Several methods are possible. One is to permit the BBFC to continue as a voluntary body working for the cinema trade and censoring films to service those cinemas who wish to stay clear of possible prosecutions and of any criticism of sexual permissiveness or excessive violence. Such an arrangement would also satisfy the desire of some of the trade to maintain a good image and to build up a reputation for largely 'family' entertainment. If, however, it were adopted by the two main cinema circuits, who

[1] *Report of the Committee on the Future of Broadcasting*, Cmnd 6753, para 16.26.

together control over a third of all cinema screens, it would allow uncensored films to be seen only where there were individual independent cinemas or film societies prepared to show them. Another possibility is for the BBFC to remain as an advisory body to the trade, monitoring films and advising on content. An informative and protective measure would be to oblige cinemas to exhibit short descriptions of the films shown in their cinemas. This policy was put forward and adopted by the GLC in the case of certain films when I was Chairman of the Film Viewing Board and was welcomed by both the Cinema Exhibitors' Association and, as far as we could judge, by the public. The object of the exercise was to let the public know what kind of film they could expect before they decided to see it. It is essential for the purpose of this exercise that the synopsis should be written in plain, objective language and that it should be placed in a prominent position inside the cinema, but that it should in no way be used as a part of sensational advertising or 'come on' appeal. We also adopted the expedient in some instances of a warning notice next to the film description which bore the words 'The GLC advises that this film contains material which may offend some people'. Although again, there is a danger that such a procedure, if not carefully controlled, could be abused for publicity purposes, its intention to warn off clients who might be upset by the film showing is surely unhelpful.

Some may argue that the controversy about film censorship is much ado about nothing. The public after all does not largely protest against the cut products shown on our screens because it does not know about the cuts. Nor, it may be argued, is the frequently distasteful material excised any great loss. Why bother to fight for the end of censorship in a small section of one area of entertainment? It is possible to argue, as Professor Bernard Crick puts it, 'Some civil liberties are more important than others'.[1]

[1] B. Crick, *Crime, Rape and Gin*, Elek/Pemberton, 1974, p. 46.

Perhaps the 'balanced' middle viewing of seeking a censorship consensus is as good a way as any to avoid all the strife and protest. Such a view seems to me to be not balanced but flabby. The middle ground is not always the right place to be, although it may seem for a time to be the safest. Even that is doubtful: Aneurin Bevan once said that those who walk down the middle of the road get run over. Asa Briggs, in his history of the BBC, comments that 'In meeting the double-fronted attack the BBC perhaps accepted too easily the simple test that if criticisms came from both left and right or from both highbrow and lowbrow, they somehow or other cancelled each other out. The test made it easy to defend the BBC in Parliament, but it did not follow that to limit argument or to promote the 'middle-brow' were proper objectives of programme policy. Cancelling out gives no guarantee of quality.'[1]

Not only quality is at stake here but liberty. Freedom is a large and grand subject but attempts to curb it may be seen in the smaller corners of our existence as well as in the bigger areas. Freedom of thought and expression, freedom to take adult decisions are all equally threatened by the vestiges of an outdated film censorship system. If we are to live free we must have the courage to face on the cinema screen what we may most fear in our inmost thought. Such is the power of film as an artistic medium that it is here that a battle still remains to be fought.

[1]A. Briggs, 'A History of Broadcasting in the UK', Vol. II, *The Golden Age of Broadcasting*, Oxford University Press, 1961, pp. 43-4.

POSTSCRIPT

Since this book was completed, there have been several pertinent developments to which reference must be made. The most significant is the appointment by the Home Secretary of a departmental committee on obscenity and film censorship under the chairmanship of Professor Bernard Williams. The setting up of the committee ends the period of Home Office stonewalling and its reliance on propping up the existing and confused system. Although there will now, no doubt, be a period when all pressures can safely be diverted by stating that the matter is under consideration by a government committee, and probably thereafter by saying that the government is still considering the Committee's report and hearing representations upon it, the setting up of the committee is a step towards the wider consideration of the controversial questions examined in this book. Moreover, the intellectual distinction of its chairman should at the least ensure that the committee's report will include some basic analysis of the right to free communications, the influence of the media on attitudes and behaviour and the extent to which the susceptibilities of the easily shocked need to be recognised and protected. It is indeed the first occasion in Britain on which there has been an official committee of enquiry into obscenity or film censorship although much of the material was the subject of evidence to the Select Committee on Obscene Publications (1958) and the Joint Committee on Censorship of the Theatre (1967).

One important contribution to the committee's deliberations will be the survey of research on *Screen Violence and Film Censorship* carried out by Stephen Brody and published as a Home Office Research Study. Brody's comprehensive survey lists some 360 research studies which have been carried out over the last 45 years with the aim of establishing what effect violence seen on the screens of cinemas and television has on viewers' attitudes and on their behaviour. The number of studies is an indication of the continuous concern over the supposedly deleterious effects of screened violence. The report states that the research does not indicate unequivocally that films and television have a socially harmful effect or that they do not. The lack of firm conclusions is attributed both to the complex nature of the questions asked and to the inadequacies of the research. For example, there is a frequent and erroneous tendency to point to correlations between, say, crime statistics and the number of violent films as evidence of a causal relationship, but the parallel existence of two trends is not in itself sufficient to say that the one causes the other.

Direct imitation of aggressive actions seen on films is said to be likely only in the case of very young children, up to the age of six or seven. The instigation of violent action following violence seen on screen is thought to be an unpredictable response confined to unusual individuals, but 'watching violent action on the screen is unlikely in itself to impel ordinary viewers to behave in ways they would otherwise not have done. That potentially violent or anti-social persons may find their own sentiments and dispositions confirmed and perhaps reinforced by television and films is not a consideration to be ignored, but it is in the amplification of existing tendencies that the main influence is likely to lie, not in the moulding of social behaviour.'[1] The study points to the comparative lack of research into peoples' emotional reactions to films of violence which may include fear and revulsion as well as identification with the characters seen. In their influence on social attitudes, films are felt to be generally superficial and unimportant, serving largely to reinforce and amplify existing views held. Certain types of audience which might be at risk to adverse influence are said to be pre-school children who may be excessively frightened or directly

[1] S. Brody, *Screen Violence and Film Censorship*. Home Office Research Study No. 40 HMSO 1977, p. 126.

imitate the actions seen, older children of impaired and immature emotional development who may identify with hero figures, and adults suffering from mental disorders or otherwise lacking firm contact with ordinary life. The Home Office survey of research does not reach conclusions which support the ready fears of the people who see in screened violence a strong argument in favour of film censorship.

However, a new contribution to the discussion has now appeared in Dr William Belson's paper to the British Association in 1977 presenting the findings of his research on *Television Violence and the Adolescent Boy*. Belson took a random sample of some 1500 boys aged 13-16 years and surveyed their television viewing since childhood with particular reference to the numbers of films with violent action they had seen. He then listed their history (as reported by them) of recent violent behaviour and looked to see whether high exposure to TV violence over the past 11 years could be correlated with serious violent behaviour. Belson's findings were 'supportive' of the view that such a correlation existed and that the two could be associated as cause and effect, and he attributed the association to the disinhibiting effects of the material seen rather than to any change in the boys' expressed attitudes or reactions to violence. This study has yet to be published in full and is based on sophisticated statistical techniques which will no doubt be evaluated by others in the field. Some doubt may well be expressed about the reliability of self-reporting by adolescent boys about their violent actions and their television viewing habits since childhood. Although Dr Belson has been careful to limit his main conclusions to support for the hypothesis he set out to examine, he firmly recommends immediate steps for a major cutback in the amount of violence shown on television and a continuing monitoring of the amount and kinds of violence shown. The jump from a 'supportive' conclusion to radical action may thus be based more on his own inclinations rather than on the strength of his research evidence.

145

Telephone
01-437 2677/8.

Telegrams :
"CENSOFILM, PHONE, LONDON."

BRITISH BOARD OF FILM CENSORS
3, SOHO SQUARE,
W.1.

PRESIDENT - THE RT. HON. THE LORD HARLECH, K.C.M.G.
SECRETARY - JOHN TREVELYAN, O.B.E.

Confidential.

5th O˅tober 19 71

Dear Sirs,

Re " NAUGHTY FILM"

I have to inform you that exception, as detailed overleaf, has been taken by the Examiners to the above film submitted by you.   The proposed category for the film is   X

Should you desire to discuss this exception form, I shall be pleased to make an appointment for this purpose at your convenience.

To Joe Bloggs Films Ltd

No.

Secretary.

British Board of Film Censors 'exception' form.

This is a true form and comments on a real film issued by the BBFC. For reasons of discretion the film company and the title of the film are invented.

EXCEPTIONS

Reel 1.   Considerably reduce the love-making between Hilde and
           a stranger, in particular removing shots and sounds
           when her head is in frame and he is making love to
           her from behind.
           Reduce to a minimum the killing of this man by Robert.

Reel 6.   The love-making between Hilde and Kerr should stop
           before we see Hilde's legs round his neck.

Reel 8.   The love-making between Monica's mother and a stranger
           should cease immediately after she throws him on the bed
           and straddles him.

Reel 9.   Reduce to a minimum the killing of this man by Monica
           and remove all sounds of his cries and the shot of
           his dead body immediately after the murder.

           Resubmit these reels.   Please mark up Reels
           1,6 & 9.

APPENDIX A

CONTROVERSIAL FILMS OF THE 1960s AND 1970s

Director	*Film Title*	*Censorship history at BBFC*
Benedek	The Wild One	BBFC certificate refused 1954, granted 1969.
Corman	The Wild Angels	BBFC cert. refused 1966. Cuts made followed by BBFC cert. 1972.
Corman	The Trip	BBFC cert. refused 1967.
Hitchcock	Psycho	BBFC cert. with cuts.
Documentary	The Warsaw Ghetto	BBFC cert. refused 1960; cuts not accepted. Excerpts shown on TV.
	The Christine Keeler Story	BBFC cert. refused 1968 and again in 1969. GLC licence refused 1970.
Kubrick	Lolita	BBFC cert. 1962. Prior consultation with BBFC.
Robbe-Grillet	Trans-Europe Express	BBFC cert. refused 1967. GLC licence refused 1967.
Sjoman	491	BBFC cert. refused 1966, GLC licence refused 1968.
Strick	Ulysses	BBFC cert. refused, GLC licence 1967.
Peckinpah	The Wild Bunch	BBFC cert. 1969 with cuts.
Sjoman	I am curious – yellow	BBFC cert. 1967 with 11 mins. cut.
Aldrich	The Killing of Sister George	BBFC cert. refused 1969. GLC licence with cuts followed by BBFC cert. with cuts.
Polanski	Rosemary's Baby	BBFC cert. with cuts 1969.
Russell	Women in Love	BBFC cert. 1969.

Director	Film Title	Censorship history at BBFC
Russell	The Devils	BBFC cert. with cuts 1971.
Corman	Bloody Mama	BBFC cert. refused, GLC licence refused, then BBFC cert. with extensive cuts 1970.
Peckinpah	Straw Dogs	BBFC cert. 1972. Prior re-editing.
Kubrick	A Clockwork Orange	BBFC cert. 1972.
Bertolucci	Last Tango in Paris	BBFC cert. 1972 with cuts.
Makavejev	W.R. – Mysteries of the Organism	BBFC cert. 1971.
Winner	The Nightcomers	BBFC cert. 1971 with cuts.
Nelson	Soldier Blue	BBFC cert. 1971 with cuts.
Jacopetti & Prosperi	Uncle Tom	BBFC cert. 1972 with cuts.
Cavani	The Night Porter	BBFC cert. 1973 with cuts.
(Film of the review)	O Calcutta	BBFC cert. refused 1972. GLC licence with cuts 1974.
(Sex education film)	Language of Love	BBFC cert. refused 1970. Licensed by GLC & other local authorities. BBFC cert. 1973. Unsuccessfully prosecuted as 'indecent'.
(Sex education film)	More about the Language of Love	BBFC cert. refused 1972. GLC licence 1974. Successfully prosecuted as 'indecent'.
Warhol/ Morrisey	Flesh	Club showing followed by police seizure, but no obscenity prosecution. BBFC cert. 1970.
Warhol/ Morrisey	Trash	BBFC cert. with cuts 1972.
Warhol/ Morrisey	Heat	BBFC cert. with cuts GLC licence uncut 1973.
Jaekin	Emmanuelle	BBFC cert. with cuts 1974.
Schatzberg	The Panic in Needle Park	BBFC cert. refused 1971, granted 1976.

Director	Film Title	Censorship history at BBFC
Animated cartoon)	Sinderella	BBFC cert. refused 1972.
(Animated cartoon)	Snow White and the Seven Perverts	BBFC cert. refused 1973. GLC licence 1973.
(Animated cartoon)	Fritz the Cat	BBFC cert. 1972
Ferreri	Blow Out (La Grande Bouffe)	BBFC proposed cuts not accepted. GLC licence uncut 1974.
Friedkin	The Exorcist	BBFC cert. 1974 with cuts.
Coppola	The Godfather	BBFC cert. 1973 with cuts.
Winner	Death Wish	BBFC cert. 1974 with cuts.
Borowcyk	Immoral Tales (Contes Immoraux)	BBFC cert. refused GLC licence 1975.
Hooper	The Texas Chain Saw Massacre	BBFC cert. refused, GLC licence 1976.
Jaekin	The Story of O (L'Histoire d'O)	BBFC cert. refused GLC licence refused 1976.
Pasolini	120 days of Sodom (Salo)	BBFC cert. refused 1977, GLC licence refused 1977. Seized at cinema club for prosecution 1977.

FILMS INSPECTED BY THE GREATER LONDON COUNCIL 1967 – 77

Year	Title	BBFC Cert.	Decision of GLC	Category
1967	Lady in a Cafe	Refused	Passed	'X' London
	Strip	Refused	Refused	—
	The Fourth Sex	Refused	Refused	—
	No. 4	Refused	Passed	'X' London
	Trans Europe Express	Refused	Refused	—
	Ulysses	Refused	Passed	'X' London
	Sexy Gang	Refused	Passed	'X' London
	The Fear	Refused	Refused	—
	I, A Woman	Refused	Passed	'X' London
	Hunger	Cuts reqd.	Passed	'X' London
	Naked Temptation	Refused	Refused	—
	Love Dossier	Refused	Refused	—
	Lust in the Swamps	Refused	Refused	—
	How much loving does a normal couple need?	Refused	Refused	—
	Aquasex	Refused	Passed	'A' London
1968	Hells Angels on Wheels	Refused	Refused	—
	The Wild Angels	Refused	Refused	—
	The Trip	Refused	Refused	—
	Bed Time	Refused	Passed	'A' London
	Because of Eve	Refused	Refused by Council	—
	Satan in High Heels	Refused	Passed	'A' London
	491	Refused	Refused	—
	Woman of Darkness	Cuts reqd.	Passed	'X' London

Year	Title	BBFC	Decision	Category
1969	Acid	Refused	Refused	—
	Sympathy for the Devil	Refused	Refused	—
	The Killing of Sister George	Cuts reqd.	Passed with cuts	'X' London
	Andrea	Refused	Refused	—
	The Molesters	Refused	Passed	'A' London
	Lorna	Refused	Refused	—
	99 Women	Refused	Refused	—
	Love Feeling	Cuts reqd.	Passed	'X' London
	Love in Our Time	Cuts reqd.	Refused	—
	Tokyo Bath Harem	Refused	Refused	—
	The Set	Cuts reqd.	Passed	'X' London
	The Wife Swappers	Refused	Refused	—
1970	The Naked Kiss	Refused	Passed	'X' London
	Shock Corridor	Refused	Passed	'X. London
	As the Naked Wind from the Sea	Refused	Refused	—
	Gisele	Refused	Refused	—
	All Together Now	Refused	Refused	—
	Zabriskie Point	Cuts reqd.	Passed	'X' London
	Love Variations	Refused	Passed	'X'
	Appointment with Lust	Refused	Refused	—
	The Christine Keeler Story	Refused	Refused	—
	Tropic of Cancer	Refused	Passed	'X'
	Satan's Sadists	Refused	Refused	—
	Bloody Mama	Refused	Refused	—
	Hotspur	Refused	Refused	—
	Marriage Manual	Refused	Refused	—

Year	Title	BBFC Cert.	Decision of Council	Category	Notes
	Anatomy of Love	Refused	Passed	X	
	Quiet Days in Clichy	Refused	Refused	—	
	Without a Stitch	Refused	Passed	X	
	Language of Love	Refused	Passed	X	Subject to cuts
1971	The Lustful Vicar	Refused	Passed	X	
	Hands off Witch	Refused	Passed	X	
	Techniques of Physical Love	Refused	Passed	X	
	Face of Terror	Refused	Refused	—	
	Man and Wife	Refused	Refused	—	
	The Daughter	Refused	Refused	—	
	Danish Value	Refused	Passed	X	
	Wonderland of Love	Refused	Refused	—	
	Karla	Refused	Refused	—	
	Virgin Witch	Refused	Passed	X	
	Camille 2000	Refused	Passed	X	
	Ripening Love	Refused	Refused	—	
	Daddy Darling	Refused	Passed	X	Subject to cut
	Trash	Refused	Refused	—	
	Succubus	Refused	Refused	—	
	The Cousins	Refused	Refused	—	
	The Big Doll House	Refused	Refused	—	
1972	Vortex	Refused	Refused	—	
	Schoolgirl Regent	Refused	Refused	—	
	Getting into Heaven	Refused	Refused	—	
	The Importance of being Sexy (Hippie-birds)	X	Passed	X	Film inspected with view to change of title

Year	Title	BBFC Cert.	Decision of Council	Category	Notes
	Sexual Freedom in Denmark	Refused	Refused	—	
	Red, White and Blue	Refused	Refused	—	
	O Calcutta	Refused	Refused	—	
1973	Together	Refused	Refused	—	
	The Porn-Brokers	Refused	Passed	X	
	Snow-white and the Seven Perverts	Refused	Passed	X	
	Is There Sex After Death?	Refused	Passed	X	
	Sex Farm	Refused	Passed	X	
	No Sex Please We're British	AA	Passed	U	Request to change category
	Schoolgirls	Refused	Refused	—	
	Love Me Deadly	Refused	Refused	—	
	Big Zapper	Refused	Refused	—	BBFC later granted X certificate with cuts
	Scorpio	X	Passed	A	Change of category
	The Girl Traders	Refused	Passed	X	Film to be called *White Slavers*
	Fist of Fury	X	No change in category	X	Request to change category
	The Sex Adventures of the Three Musketeers	Refused	Passed	X	
	Manson	Refused	Passed	X	Film description
	Blow-out	Refused	Passed	X	Warning notice and film description
	Heat	X	Passed	X	Without cuts imposed by BBFC. Film description
	Quiet Days in Clichy	Refused	Passed	X	Reinspection. Warning notice and film description

153

Year	Title	BBFC Cert.	Decision of Council	Category	Notes
	Bay of Blood	Refused	Refused	—	
	Mark of the Devil	Refused	Refused	—	
1974	The Telephone Book	Refused	Refused	—	
	Toilet Talks	Refused	Passed	X	
	O Calcutta	Refused	Passed	X	Warning notices and film description
	Techniques of Love	Refused	Passed	X	
	More About the Language of Love	Refused	Passed	X	
	Teenage Love	Refused	Passed	X	
	Prison Girls	Refused	Passed	X	
	The Bloody Fists	Refused	Passed subject to cuts	X	
	Events	Refused	Passed		
	City of Sin	Refused	Refused	—	
	The Demons	Refused	Passed	X	Warning notice
	Ain't Misbehavin'	Refused	Passed	X	
	Chinese Hercules	Refused	Refused	—	
	How to Seduce A Virgin	Refused	Passed	X	
1975	Les Valseuses	Refused	Passed	X	
	Score	Refused	Passed	X	
	La Bonzesse	Refused	Passed	X	
	The Dirty Mind of Young Sally	Refused	Passed	AA	
	Immoral Stories	Refused	Passed	X	
	Punishment	Refused	Refused	—	
1976	Best of New York Erotic Film Festival	Refused	Passed	X	
	Violated Angels	Refused	Refused	—	

Year	Title	BBFC Cert.	Decision of Council	Cate-gory	Notes
	My 'X' Wife	Refused	Refused	—	
	Exhibition	Refused	Passed	X	
	Pussy Talk	Refused	Passed	X	
	Last House on the Left	Refused	Refused	—	
	Texas Chainsaw Massacre	Refused	Passed	X	Warning notices
	Wet Dreams	Refused	Passed	X	
	Woman's Best Friend	Refused	Passed	X	
	The Story of 'O'	Refused	Refused	—	
	Gatekeeper's Daughter	Refused	Passed	X	
	The Coming of Seymour	Refused	Refused	—	
	I Love You, I Don't	Refused	Passed	X	
1977	120 Days of Sodom	Refused	Refused	—	
	The Private Afternoons of Pamela Mann	Refused	Passed	X	
	Maitresse	Refused	Refused	—	
	4 Days of Love	Refused	Refused	—	

SELECT BIBLIOGRAPHY

Official Publications

Joint Committee on Censorship of the Theatre: Report H.L. 255 H.C. 503, HMSO 1967.

The Law Commission (Law Com. No. 76): Report on Conspiracy and Criminal Law Reform,HMSO 1976.

S. Brody: Screen Violence and Film Censorship – A Review of Research, Home Office Research Study No. 40, HMSO 1977.

Greater London Council: The Future of Film Censorship for Adults, AR 741 and 742, October 1974 (Committee reports).

Report of the Commission on Obscenity and Pornography, U.S. Government Printing Office 1967. (A summarised account of the main report is given in *The Obscenity Report*, Olympia Press 1971)

Television and Growing Up: The Impact of Televised Violence, Report to the Surgeon General's Scientific Advisory Committee on Television and Social Behaviour, U.S. Government Printing Office 1972.

Violence and the Media, Report to the National Commission on the Causes and Prevention of violence, U.S. Government Printing Office 1969.

Other Publications

Arts Council of Great Britain: The Obscenity Laws, Report of the Working Party. Andre Deutsch 1969.

Fraser, John: Violence in the Arts. Cambridge University Press 1971.

Halloran, J.D., Brown, R.L., Chaney, D.C.: Television and Delinquency. Leicester University Press 1970.

Holbrook, David: The Pseudo-Revolution. Tom Stacey 1972.

Jowell, Roger, Spence, James and Shaheen, Gutrez: Film Censorship Exploratory Study. Social and Community Planning Research 1974.

Longford, Lord: Pornography: The Longford Report. Coronet Books 1972.

McQuail, Denis (ed): The Sociology of Mass Communications. Penguin 1972.

O'Higgins, Paul: Censorship in Britain. Nelson 1972.

Phelps, Guy: Film Censorship. Gollancz 1975.

Trevelyan, John: What the Censor Saw. Michael Joseph 1973.

INDEX